Comments about the Divination Workbook

I am pleased with the accuracy of the information you provided and how it works for me! I've always been rather intuitive but now I amaze my family and friends with my accuracy regarding lost things and insight about people.

Jill Peterson
Baltimore, Maryland

The Divination Workbook honestly changed my life. It is a must read for everyone who seeks and loves truth. I believe your work will shift our global consciousness about truth, as it has shifted mine.

Steven Solin
San Diego, California

An inspiration catalyst, your workbook is a remarkable collection of practical and spiritual applications to facilitate lifelong learning.

Sherrol McCabe
New York

A true visionary tool, guiding us towards a new, more wholesome millennium of attunement with the divine within us all.

Sally Schultz
Taos, New Mexico

This book by Rev. Iris K Barratt will help you through the biggest pitfall in all spiritual practice; that is, the ego wants to come in and turn your spiritual practice into ego practice. Iris teaches you how to come from a place beyond the ego, so your action, decisions, and insights come out of your true spiritual nature.

Tom Pritscher
Director, Bald Mountain Meditation Center, Idaho

A golden opportunity to awaken to and work with the processes of the universe for the benefit of everyone!

Trisha Goodall
St. Mary, Kentucky

As a Libran, I had difficulty making decisions and sticking to them. Thanks to your practical guide I now make decisions quickly and easily. I'm not sure who is happiest about my changes, me or my family! Thank you!

Pat Windsor
Naples, Florida

Rev. Barratt's insight into the soul's power offers an excellent opportunity to better utilize what comes naturally to us all. This exceptional workbook is a necessary companion along our pathway to the truth.

Linda Mae Hieter
President, Intermountain Regional Learning Center

You have greatly assisted me in taking risks with confidence and letting go of old fearful thinking. Your wisdom and insights have assisted me in taking positive action and making many important new changes.

Jenifer Mc Bride
Austin, Texas

As a virtual novice in matters of the heart and soul, your book has inspired me to listen to my own inner wisdom which helps me cope with the complexities of my overly analytical mind. I now enjoy a sense of balance, skill and faith I never knew before.

Joseph Ellsworth
Ontario, Canada

I taught my granddaughter Iris as a child, yet for many years now she has been my greatest teacher. She is honestly a miracle worker of amazing faith and skill. I have seen it many times. She is a living example of living in harmony with one's true spiritual awareness.

Edith Mellen
Salt Lake City, Utah

Rev. Iris K. Barratt's

Divination Workbook

An Expert's Guide to Awakening the Power and Wisdom of Your Soul

SECOND REVISED EDITION

www.arttoday.com"

Awakening Visions Publishing
Sun Valley, Idaho USA

Divination Workbook;

An Expert's Guide to Awakening the Power and Wisdom of Your Soul.
Published by Awakening Visions, P.O. Box 80, Bellevue, Idaho 83313 U.S.A.
Second Edition, Revised

This hardcover edition of the *Divination Workbook* features a
"self jacket" that eliminates the need for a separate dust jacket. It provides
sturdy protection for your book while it saves paper, trees and energy.

First Printing, 1998
Second Printing 1999, Revised
Includes Bibliographical references and Index

ISBN, 1-893087-03-4
Library of Congress Cataolg Number: 98-97016

Disclaimer

This workbook is designed to provide information in regards to the subject matter covered. It is sold with the understanding that the publisher and author are not engaged in rendering legal, medical or scientific advice. If expert assistance is required, the services of a competent professional should be sought.

It is not the purpose of this manual to reprint all the information that is otherwise available to the author, but to compliment, amplify and supplement other texts. You are urged to read all the available material, learn as much as possible about divination and pendulum skills and to tailor the information to your individual needs.

For your information, see the many references in the Appendix. The purpose of this manual is to educate and entertain. The author and Awakening Visions Publishing shall have neither liability nor responsibility to any person or entity with respect to any loss or damage caused, alleged to be caused, directly or indirectly by the information contained in this book. If you do not wish to be bound by the above, you may return this book to the publisher for a full refund. Thank you.

Awakening Visions Publishing
"Enhancing Educational and Cultural Diversity"
Personal Development/Divination
P.O. Box 80
Bellevue, Idaho 83313 U.S.A.
email <visionpb@micron.net>
WebPage: http://www.awakeningvisions.com

FOREWORD

Reverend Iris K. Barratt has written a new workbook on pendulum divination, a wonderfully practical and insightful book that outlines the techniques necessary to master pendulum divination and dowsing easily and correctly. She is especially qualified to do this because of her vast knowledge of divination, dowsing, private investigating, peacemaking, and various spiritual practices, together with her background and training in clinical hypnotherapy for many years.

This book is a personal, spiritual guide on how, in these challenging times, to enrich one's life in hundreds of ways. It is an inspirational catalyst to your own questions, intuition and vision.

As a brilliant and fearless leader and peace activist, Rev. Iris K. Barratt challenges each individual to lead a spiritually rewarding life and then shows the reader how to do it with traditional and unique pendulum divination and dowsing techniques. This workbook proves to be an incredible tool, an excellent, simple and practical course for getting to know your "SELF," again and again.

As an experienced and effective counselor, Iris assists the reader to meet these practical and spiritual challenges by showing how to ask the right questions and locate the most harmonious path to successful resolutions both ***within*** the mind, body and soul and ***without***, into one's personal world. I believe that Iris has written a very clear and understandable book that enhances the practicality and spirituality of the phenomenon of divining techniques.

Each and every reader will find abundant practical uses for this workbook. It is certain to be of outstanding service as a real self-help to anyone interested in the fields of divination, dowsing, investigations, hypnosis, personal or spiritual enrichment. This workbook offers practical public benefit, which is perhaps, the most important criteria to consider for any endeavor.

Reverend Stacie Sharp
The Planet Peace Project

ACKNOWLEDGMENTS

I would like to acknowledge all of my teachers and students, all seekers and intuitives of the past, present and future, for their willingness and courage to confront the challenges of life's unknown possibilities and ask, *What if?*

I would like to acknowledge everyone who loves and seeks the truth, be it personal, social, spiritual or universal in nature.

I would like to thank the following people, with deepest gratitude, for being the supportive blessings which they continue to be in my life:

Michael L. Barratt (my beloved husband)
Leah Austin (my precious daughter for her editing and layout skills)
Rev. Stacie Sharp
The Planet Peace Project
Jessica Jacobsen
Linda Mae Hieter
Patrick E. Reilly
Frank Jordan, Master Dowser
Claire Lodahl and family
Master Tom Pritscher, Bald Mountain Meditation Center
Lissa K. Austin (my other precious daughter)
Edith Lehman Mellen (my precious grandmother)
David Yurth, Ph.D.
Lisa Sedivy and The Blaine County School District
Rev. Ruth Hoppe, Dr. Louis Allen and all of my fellow peaceniks!

Contents

Contents Continued

CHAPTER NINE: Children

CHAPTER TEN: Education and Research

CHAPTER ELEVEN: Family and Relationships

CHAPTER TWELVE: Health and Wellness

Contents Continued

"Divination is cultivation of your sensitivity to associative, intuitive and spiritual clues, which expands your capacity for making accurate and meaningful assessments.

Divination is simply a matter of training yourself to be more aware of and sensitive to the signals already present within every aspect of your existence.

Divination is using these insights for your own benefit and the benefit of others. It facilitates practical communication with the cosmos." Rev. Iris K Barratt

"Learning is finding out what you already know.
Doing is demonstrating that you know it.
Teaching is reminding others that
they know it just as well as you.
You are all learners, doers, teachers."

Richard Bach, Illusions

Author's Introduction
Your Visionary Quest

I once heard a true story about a young visionary or seeker of truth, who felt very in tune with a spiritual master from India. The master would appear in the seekers dreams and seemed to fill them with love and insight. After careful planning the seeker finally went to India to see this master and gain the answers to the many questions that invaded the visionary's mind. Once in India the seeker followed the master around, sure this enlightened being had the answers. The master was always surrounded by many people and generally the seeker got only smiles from the master instead of answers. When the seeker's time had run out, the master was approached and literally begged in desperation for the answers.

The master looked lovingly at the seeker and said, "I'll give you the answer in one statement." The seeker was overjoyed and with great attention, listened for the answer. The master smiled and lovingly said, ***"It is not a rational process!"*** The seeker was stunned, angry, and wondering what kind of answer is that? Later however, at a calmer moment, the seeker pondered, "If it is not a rational process, then I wonder what it is?" Thus began the process of illumination for the seeker.

I love this story because I relish the great mysteries of life, like divination and spiritual awakening, which elude my scientific, rational mentality! I always relish the magical and miraculous experiences of healing, transcendent awakening, and enlightenment. For as long as I can remember, I have felt drawn to every type of divination tool and experience. Yes, I have witnessed many miraculous experiences in my life and although my logical mind has always wondered about **the why and how** of it all, I have learned to honor the mystery of synchronicity and guidance. My life is largely about claiming the powers of divinity, divination, healing, and the evolution of consciousness, yours, mine, and ours. I have taught prayer, forgiveness, divination, and hypnotherapy (healing, investigation and evolution techniques) to physicians, investigators, engineers, and other analytical personalities, for many years. I have grown weary of attempting to defend and define the magic of spiritual divinity, and the numerous modalities of divination, that often lie beyond the rational mind.

Albert Einstein said it best, "...great spirits have always encountered violent opposition from mediocre minds." While I honor and respect science, my objective is not to exalt or undermine it, but to enhance it with awareness of our divinity and soul evolution. I clearly see the divinity in science and scientists, I honor their quest to understand the dynamics of our natural world. I clearly see the divinity in medicine and physicians, I honor their quest to heal, cure and ease suffering. Therefore, this book is about moving beyond an *either/or* mentality to one of inclusiveness. While I risk discussing my personal theories and views about divination and dowsing from a logical perspective, I continue to embrace the "Great Mystery."

Through my interests in hypnotherapy and private investigations, I have studied copious amounts of information about integrating logic and intuition, conscious and subconscious. I always find myself wondering about the soul and how soul awareness fits into the whole picture of evolution, both in terms of consciousness and physical manifestation. As a clinical hypnotherapist, I often wonder if many of the powers attributed to the subconscious mind are really attributes, or powers of the soul level of awareness. Before I ever dreamed about being a healer who uses hypnotherapy, I felt frustrated by the typical hypnotist or dowser who says, "We don't know how or why the subconscious mind works to evoke such powerful changes."

I have always felt that the soul is responsible for our most powerful changes, as it responds to both elevated thoughts and feelings. Enhancing soul awareness is the focus of the many divination techniques I use and teach in my life. I always seem to intuitively know that hypnosis is like prayer, meditation, and divination: a clear reflection of our soul level of awareness, and our divine connection to the whole of consciousness.

My visionary or mystical quest has challenged me to wonder:

What if the magic of divination could be explained by understanding our divinity, and our soul connection to the divine?

What if the soul is neither spirit nor matter, but is the relationship between them?

What if our soul, therefore encompasses spirit, (etheric body) matter, (physical body), personality, thoughts, mental and emotional intelligence, and therefore the soul constitutes one great totality of being?

What if the soul is the basis of vitality, which underlies every form and links all parts together and is a fact of nature?

What if the soul could be defined as that significant aspect in every form, (made through the union of spirit and matter), which feels, registers awareness, attracts and repels, responds or denies response and keeps all form in a state of vibrational activity?

What if the soul is what mystics have referred to as the sacred web of life?

What if divination and dowsing are explained by our soul connection which includes the whole known universe, the earth, sun, stars and all of creation, and transcends physical time and space?

What if the soul is the force of evolution itself?

What if the spiritual approach to divination is the scientific approach?

I believe a paradigm shift in awareness must move us from the *either/or* mentality to one of inclusiveness, to finding the underling unity between all things, as reflected in our souls awareness. This unity includes science and spirituality, logic and intuition, medicine and transpersonal healing which transcends time and space. I am very grateful for the opportunity to share with you such a wide variety of processes, that have truly transformed my life! My hope is that this workbook will inspire you to ask your own questions, divine your own answers, claim your personal power by making friends with power, and enhance the evolution of your soul. I honor and bless your visionary quest. You may enjoy my definition of a visionary: One who is gratefully inspired and haunted by humanitarian ideals! Sound familiar?

I have done my best to create a variety of both practical and transpersonal applications that will lead you to an enhanced awareness of a spiritually oriented universe in process.

The Search for Certainty in an Uncertain World

We live in a world of uncertainty with countless variables to constantly consider. Each problem or challenge that we face in our daily lives has an element of risk. The most common fear is "fear of the unknown." One of our greatest challenges is learning to trust our instincts. Many animals have developed this capacity to a very high degree in order to insure survival. Our search for true security can seem endless, both within our world and within ourselves.

What about people? How many of us are in tune with our instincts, our intuition, or our soul awareness? Science has clearly demonstrated that magnetic theory indicates there is either neutral, attractive, or repulsive energy between all things. To insure survival, and to evolve, all living organisms have needed to sense these energies and gravitate towards the positive, beneficial ones and avoid the negative, destructive ones. Most people have developed this ability unconsciously although they are not always aware of it. We often miss, or ignore, what we are experiencing at deeper levels of our awareness. We are often in *"Brain Drain,"* and therefore not evolving our physical, mental, emotional, or spiritual intelligences. This inner knowing of spirit, or divine intelligence, is registered through your mind, soul and nervous system. This is the communication system of your body.

The successes in my life have had less to do with my ego knowing all the answers and more to do with learning to ask the right questions and attuning to and listening for my spiritual guidance. This is what has inspired the publishing of this workbook: being a student and honoring the life force of Spirit or Divinity. A Visionary Quester (to me) is one who actively investigates and participates in their life's quest. One who chooses to ask their own questions and create their own sacred blessings, prayers, or rituals. One who participates in loving and intelligent co-creation and peacemaking. These choices have a rich history within most cultures.

Pendulum divination is an ancient, powerful tool, that can guide you to discover and effectively use the three primary energies of positive, negative and neutral, to literally search and find anything. Divination can lead you to more trust and certainty in a uncertain world! This workbook will allow you to become a more conscious co-creator or one who creates together with divine guidance. You will learn to become more clear about your intentions and the causes and effects of your life. You will learn more self trust, which is the foundation of inner knowing. Personal and spiritual awareness is often gained most directly through inner work or inner transformation. Being important enough to ask, and divine enough to be answered, is truly putting your life in the hands of spiritual guidance. Divination is the creative guesswork of the inquisitive, evolving soul. Only by participating will you discover your own truth!

Claiming Your Powers of Divinity and Divination

Divinity may be defined as, the state or quality of being divine, as a God, Goddess, Spirit, or Angel. Divinity is present in humans as the spiritual or transpersonal aspect of human nature--the Divine within. Expressed another way, Divinity provides the source of intuition, conscience, and revelation of truth to us.

Divination, or the art of divining, may be defined as, practicing certain activities in order to predict future events, obtain secret knowledge, or reveal the truth through contact with divine sources, omens, or oracles, or by means of inspiration, intuition, or reflection.

Divination has many names and many forms. In ancient Rome it was referred to as ***augury*** and practiced by professionals. Their function was to predict what was in store for others, and to advise them on future issues. Some types of divination occur spontaneously such as common intuitive hunches, a strong sense of knowing, inner sight or clairvoyance, inner hearing or clairaudience, or inner sensations or clairsentience.

People who use divination have historically made use of external physical instruments or modalities to assist them in penetrating the veil or unknown. Divination is an ancient means of obtaining both practical and spiritual insights, and is a powerful tool to meet the demanding needs of our fast-paced modern age. Divination modalities used today reflect both ancient, historical, and contemporary methods. These include: numbers, cards, mirrors, hands, stars, crystals, water, books, stones, pearls, pendulums, rods, urine, animals, dreams, oracles, moles, sticks and others. For information regarding the history of divination and dowsing, I recommend, The Divining Hand, by Christopher Bird. Bird has created a well researched book which encompasses many excellent historical examples of dowsing's credibility, and accuracy.

I'd like to share what divination is like for me personally, *without* the need for a pendulum or visual symbol. I trust that some of these experiences are true for you also! Divination is about feeling open and aware of the synchronicity and timing of events, thoughts, or feelings. It is being aware of the confirmations and coincidences. It's like sitting outside under a tree, writing, and feeling the horses staring at you from across the pasture, and looking up to find this to be true and waving good morning. Divination is soulfully anticipating the needs of others accurately, and with perfect timing. It is being present and tuning in, asking to be a neutral witness, to experience soulful understanding, for the highest good of all concerned. It's saying the same thing as your friend at the same time.

Divination is your willingness to gratefully witness the patterns, connections, and confirmations in your life and the lives of others. It is believing that your soul is connected to all of the causes and effects, events and experiences, of life. It's like standing in the warm sun on a perfect Spring day, seeing and feeling the new growth of life in so many beautiful forms, patterns, and connections. It's remembering that your soul responds to love, healing and wholeness. It's trusting that life-affirming elements, like air and vitamins from the sun, exist, even if you can't see them. Divination is trusting your first feeling, when you have lost your sunglasses, as you tune-in, to remember where they are.

Divination is trusting that everything is connected on a soul level, where you know more than you generally know or recognize. Self-trust is the foundation for inner knowing, and as you generate confirmations which reflect your trust, your inner knowing and accuracy increase. In conclusion, divination is the art or act of inner knowledge which can enhance your life in many ways.

What is Dowsing?

Dowsing is a type of divination primarily used to find external objects rather than information. Dowsing is also referred to as radiation physics, radionics or radiesthesia. The most well known use of dowsing has probably been to find water with the aid of a willow stick, commonly known as water witching. Divination and dowsing can be used by anyone to literally search for and find anything, from general information to actual physical things such as lost persons or stolen property. This is evident in my classes where students imagine or pretend that they can ask and know, and to their amazement they discover they can! For centuries the process of dowsing has been used by miners, investigators, the military, and others to locate things of importance.

What is a Pendulum?

For our purposes, a pendulum is any object suspended (hung) from a string or chain and held between the thumb and forefinger. The pendulum is a visual aid used to measure both inner and outer energies, vibrations and electromagnetic force fields. Some texts say it was discovered by Galileo in 1583, others report that ancient Egyptians used it long before. The pendulum is considered by divination and dowsing experts to be the most versatile tool because it is so easily constructed, transported, and because its applications for gaining information are virtually unlimited. The pendulum is commonly used to witness and measure the three basic spiritual energies of the universe: positive, negative and neutral. Have you ever seen someone use a ring or some other object, suspended by a string and held over an expectant mother to discern if the unborn baby will be a boy or a girl? This is a common example of pendulum divination.

One day while I was hiking, I needed a pendulum. Necessity then became the mother of invention, and I created a very funny looking pendulum. A small five year old boy named Tony was missing. He was last seen wearing green shorts, a blue shirt and black tennis shoes. Everyone was frantically racing in different directions. I wondered what I might have in my backpack to use as a pendulum to discern the direction Tony had taken. As I quickly looked through my pack, there it was! Perfectly symmetrical, natural cotton, suspended by a cotton string, perfect, a tampon! I unwrapped it, soaked it with water to straighten it out and add more weight and then I began. I took a deep relaxing breath and begin facing each direction and asking, "Is little Tony out in this direction?" I got positive responses from the north and east. I started running, with my dog leading the way, and found a main northeastern trail. I ran through the woods, calling and found Tony in about fifteen minutes, joyfully playing with a stick in the creek. Thank goodness I was prepared with my pendulum skills. No one seemed to care what tool I had used to locate this child. We all just smiled a lot!

How Pendulum Divination Can Transform Your Life!

Through your willingness to use the techniques presented in this workbook, you can:

- Become skilled in basic and advanced pendulum divination techniques
- Gain insights which can be 100% accurate
- Discern the most favorable course of action in any area of your life
- Discover limitless creative insights
- Fine-tune your ability to ask the most pertinent questions
- Discover your own truth and enhance your self-trust
- Access awareness of a creative, expansive and process-oriented universe
- Explore transpersonal (non-ordinary or spiritual) modes of consciousness (such as intuition, telepathy, clairvoyance, hypnotic trances, meditation, spiritual insights and spiritual experiences)
- Sharpen your visionary skills and enhance your timing and synchronicity
- Discover new perspectives and choices regarding any situation
- Experience the power of decisive decision-making
- Save time, money, and energy in every aspect of your life
- Become more efficient and productive in all your endeavors
- Become a conscious co-creator, or one who creates together with divine guidance
- Create healing miracles in your life and / or the lives of others
- Learn to become more clear about your intentions, and the causes and effects of your life
- Discover the peace, joy, and freedom of soul attunement, awareness and evolution (Honest! You can do it! You **are** it!)

Using these fun, practical exercises can provide accurate and insightful information, that can truly transform every area of your life. A person skilled in basic pendulum techniques, aligned with neutrality and the highest intentions, can gain insights which are 100% accurate. These pendulum responses literally show the most favorable course of action in any area of questioning. They facilitate alignment with higher will, mind, and heart, through embracing the soulful, neutral, or middle way. Hypnotic trances and divination are, and have been universally present as tools for tapping into the subconscious and superconscious, and gaining soul awareness. If imagination and awareness are unlimited, so are your opportunities for personal and spiritual insight. Perhaps the most powerful aspect of these exercises is the opportunity they provide to actively participate in your own personal and spiritual evolution. No one else can do it for you! I equate this to the vital importance of participating in your own healing process, as all healing is ultimately self-healing.

You learn to get out of the way, in the negative sense, and participate in the positive sense. Only you can evolve and manifest your loving intentions, personal power and healing. This workbook will serve as your catalyst. These are your questions and you are the quester. It is your healing and you are the healer. It is your vision and you are the visionary. Discover your own truth and align it with Universal Truth! Learn this powerful new skill and claim your personal power by being part of the solution. Quantum physics suggests that our conscious choices have a direct, demonstrable effect on the way creation manifests in every moment.

"Learning is the beginning of wealth.
Learning is the beginning of health.
Learning is the beginning of spirituality.
Searching and learning is where the miracle process all begins."
Jim Rohn ~ (American Businessman, Author, Speaker, Philosopher)

Why Does Pendulum Divination Work?

There have been many explanations about how divination works throughout history. When first introduced to this method of investigation, which has always defied rational explanations, most people react with blatant disbelief. Divination, however, is one of the mental abilities called "psychic," which promises a revolutionary advance in human communication with the cosmos surrounding us.

My personal experience is that divination works because we live in a universe of Spirit (Divine Spiritual Intelligence) sometimes referred to as the "web of life." This web of life is the basis of vitality, and is another name for our soul connection to universal consciousness. Divination is commonly thought to work because we all have access to three levels of mind, emotions, and experiences which reflect this web of life. They are commonly referred to as: conscious, subconscious, and superconscious.

The Conscious Mind

The conscious aspect of mind is the everyday logical, thinking faculty. It is also known as the analytical, critical faculty. Your logic is what gets you through the day, makes sure you are on track, and refers you back to experience when needed. Logic (Conscious Mind) is taught to ask intelligent questions by analyzing the past.

The Subconscious Mind

The subconscious controls the involuntary functions of the body (breathing, heartbeat, illness, healing, growth, etc.) It also, controls our basic instincts, and is the habitual, or automatic portion of our mental and emotional processes, of which we are unaware. Subconscious memories, or processes, can come into awareness in many ways, such as dreams, hypnosis, contemplation, trances, or specific divination questioning. Your subconscious mind is considered to be the gateway to your intuition, soul awareness, and superconscious (the universal mind).

The Superconscious Mind

The superconscious aspect of mental and emotional intelligence is the highest or fully spiritual aspect of consciousness. It is connected to the oversoul, defined as, spiritual essence or vital force in the universe in which all souls participate, which transcends individual consciousness. It is attunement and enlightenment, where miracles that transcend time and space occur. It is where one can tap into the Akashic records (the cosmic or universal memory system reflecting all that is, all that was, and all that ever will be). This is also where past life memories are thought to originate. It is also referred to as the universal mind.

"Nothing is impossible for the human soul which strives to elevate itself. It is strong because of its ties with other souls which are its kindred." White Brotherhood

Attunement and Soul Evolution

Attunement means to bring oneself into spiritual harmony. It is what experts believe accounts for the selectivity in divination. Attunement is the process of focusing on the specific question at hand and tuning out all else. Attunement reflects soul energy, or the sacred web of life. Due to the basic unity of all creation, and a resonance between octaves of frequency, it is possible for human consciousness to attune itself to other levels of consciousness. The microcosmic, in attunement with the macrocosmic frequency, will resonate in harmonic response. The spiritual law, "***As above, so below*** " reflects this truth. Being ***"On the same wavelength"*** is a familiar expression for attunement.

To attune to neutral divination trance, using the subconscious and superconscious, we use trance language. Trance language is a term used by hypnotherapists who work with transpersonal (non-ordinary and perfectly natural) levels of consciousness. Using trance language means we can ask for anything we want that Spirit, God (or the highest good of all concerned) supports. We can co-create with spiritual intelligence and expect miracles of healing or attunement. Anything good becomes possible! We ask, ***What if*** I could create for the highest good for all concerned and enhance global healing? ***What if*** I could locate the best possible outcome regarding any situation? ***What if*** I could feel gratitude and love and circulate it with positive statements of blessing? ***What if*** it would be fun and interesting to do my best and test the results? In sacred trance language, used in prayer, divination, or ritual, we can choose to make positive choices to give and receive. We can ask questions, listen, and assimilate the answers.
Ask yourself:
"What does serving the highest good means to me?"
"What examples of intuition and guidance do I recognize in my life?"

The following practices, are all examples of utilizing the communication abilities of our mind, soul and nervous system- prayer, meditation, hypnotherapy, kinesiology, iridology, neurology, acupuncture, reflexology, palmistry (our lines are manifestations of energy, formed by the brain and through the nervous system and are in a constant state of change), soul healing, and divination.

"You are important enough to ask, and Divine enough to be answered."
Ramtha

You are encouraged to write your own questions, statements, blessings or prayers and give and receive what you will. As in all skills, what really matters in the end is your knowledge and awareness. Divination is an excellent reflection of your current state of consciousness. Accuracy reflects alignment with the vertical path, neutrality, clear intentions and questions, as well as attunement and focus. Since divination is actually you working on a soul level, everything you do, think, feel, and expect is part of the context and is the most challenging part to bring under your direction.

What do you want to ask? What do you choose to give or receive right now? What do you want to attune to and resonate with? When asking these questions one should consider the law of karma.

The Law of Karma and Resonance

Karma is a Sanskrit word that literally means action. The basic law of karma has come to mean action and reaction, or cause and effect. Karma is the force that leads to reincarnation. Destiny is a synonym for karma. In any one life we plant the seeds of the personality that will grow during that and subsequent lifetimes. Every soul has free will, or freedom of choice. A law of retribution extends over the entire karmic cycle. All of our lessons are recorded in our Akashic records or the oversoul, and are used to determine the quality and challenges of each of our new lives. These records are the sum total of our past, present and future lives and are accessible through our superconscious mind or the soul. Karma neither rewards nor punishes, as it reflects neutrality and unconditional love. This universal law of cause and effect gives meaning to all attitudes, intentions, and actions.

Our karmic subcycles are influenced by our attitudes and intentions, the law of sympathetic vibrations, or resonance. What we give out energetically will be returned to us! Like attracts like! The soul is defined as an entity which is regarded as being the eternal, or spiritual part, of the person. Though having no physical or material reality, it is credited with the functions of thinking and willing, hence determining all behavior. The soul is the essence of our being. The soul manifests as an extension of consciousness. The soul qualities are brought into play through the interplay of opposites, spirit and matter, and their effects upon each other. This is the basis of consciousness. Exploring your own self-awareness, accessing your higher self or soul and raising the quality of your soul's energy is the basis of spiritual growth, healing, and taking control of your life.

By understanding the law of sympathetic vibrations or resonance, ***like attracts like***, one can fully understand the power of forgiveness. When we gain compassion for ourselves and others and choose to move forward by practicing forgiveness, we will receive what we give. It is because like attracts like that miracles of forgiveness abound, whether you recognize them or not.

Forgiveness is a gift of peace that you can give to yourself and others. Although it is ***not*** considered a rational process by most people, it reflects understanding "Good Karma." Meditation is also an ancient, powerful practice for moving beyond cause and effect into being and oneness. For exploring the practice of meditation, I highly recommend, Practicing the Presence: A Course in Meditation, by Tom Pritscher. Tom has created an excellent, simple, and practical course for learning to go beyond thought and concept, into practicing the Source or Presence in every moment.

When we think of cause and effect, we're thinking in terms of time. Whatever we describe as the 'cause' always occurs before its 'effect.' Cause and effect are seen as cycles or patterns in time. All physical events, the effects of causes, are patterns that allow us to see them in a synchronistic or predictive way. Understanding causality (cause and effect) and acausality (patterns which occur outside of time and space or without cause) leads us to the techniques of divination, dowsing and long distance healing. Whatever causes these processes to work exists beyond the concepts of cause and effect, time or space. Divination involves becoming grateful and humble and asking to serve the highest good, doing so, and watching the synchronicity and miracles increase exponentially (not limited by time or space). Can you trust that your soul remembers how to serve consciousness when given the opportunity? Can you trust that it may not be a rational process and that perhaps the mind creates the abyss and the heart crosses it?

A Visionary Future, What if-

Can you envision what future applications the mysteries of divination holds for humanity in exploring other energy sciences and the farthest reaches of universal consciousness?

What if pendulum divination can:

...determine if a person is telling the truth

...determine the best type of rehabilitation

...determine the exact locations of anyone or anything

...transform private, social and transpersonal investigations

...transform our health care systems

...diagnose any imbalances

...assist choosing the most healing treatments and remedies

...eliminate exploratory surgery with humane divining techniques

...minimize the costs of health care

...facilitate healing which transcends both time and space

...assist giving and receiving

...assist soul awareness and evolution

When everyone claims the ability to ask and receive personal guidance for diagnosis of any imbalances, and then chooses the most beneficial healing treatment or remedy, the world could then resonate with individual and collective health and wellness. Through exploration of precise information regarding physical symptoms, psychological and emotional aspects of patients, we can more easily treat the true causes of illness. The true focus and function of every healer is to treat each patient wholistically.

By using pendulum skills, we can diagnose the vibration and vitality of every system or part of the body. We can reveal the precise disorders through maps and lists, be they physical, psychological, emotional, or any combination thereof. It is my hope that through using these methods of fine-tuning, exploratory surgery will no longer exist and the costs of health care will be minimized. Color and sound therapies can compliment other modern medical treatments. Colors and sounds are energies with specific wavelengths and frequencies which affect our chakras, or energy systems. Our energy bodies, or auras, are composed of all the colors of the rainbow, and a balance can be maintained for optimal health and well-being.

It is when we start from the center, vertical path of neutrality, spirit or oneness, that we can manifest the most beneficial causes and effects in healing and all other co-creation. We can find the inner resources of life, love and truth within neutrality and polarity, enabling us to use our powers of discernment constructively.

I believe these possibilities can and will happen when we restore our consciousness to the sacred dynamics of a spiritual energy universe in process, which is Spirit or God in limitless manifestation. Pendulum communications with our sub and superconscious aspects of mind and soul is a powerful tool, which can lead us to practical personal empowerment and expanded spiritual consciousness.

This workbook is meant to serve as a foundation, guide and catalyst to your infinite questions and applications. It is my hope that you will create even more meaningful questions and more diverse personal and spiritual applications. I honor your visionary quest. You are a unique being, an important part of all our evolution. No one else could ever take your place!

"She/he who wishes to show us a truth should place us in a situation where we will discover it for ourselves."

-Ortega y Gasset,
Meditations on Quixote

Preparing for Accurate Pendulum Communications

Our conscious, subconscious, and superconscious faculties serve us in our questioning and answering processes. The pendulum serves as a visual tool to enhance communication between these aspects of mind. Your conscious mind formulates and asks the questions and the neutral sub and superconscious aspects of mind or soul awareness measures and reports the answers through the neuromuscular system. Then your conscious mind evaluates the responses and fine-tunes the questioning process. Your mind's capacity for sending and receiving information is totally awe inspiring, both scientifically and in terms of unexplained phenomena. Scientifically or energetically, the mind has the ability to ask and receive neutral and polarized energy responses through the neuromuscular system. Some believe it is through the biblical emphasis on powers of the spoken word and asking to receive that the mysteries of divining powers are understood. I met a member of The Canadian Society of Questers who feels this very strongly. He could care less about polarity, electromagnetic force fields or scientific theory, and concerns himself only with the belief that we have the inherent right through our divinity, or our functioning spiritual self or soul, to ask and receive anything that Spirit or God wills for us to know. Your subconscious mind must first be prepared or programmed for accurate communication responses.

Constructing your own pendulum

Popular items for constructing pendulums include: natural woods, crystals, gemstones, metal bolts, and personal items like rings or necklaces. For best results, use something symmetrical (the same shape on both sides). Hang your pendulum from a chain or string about six inches long. I prefer using a wooden pendulum suspended by a cotton string. With experience, you will discover what length of chain or string, and what kind of object you prefer.

Gaining Mastery of Your Subconscious Resources

You must understand that your subconscious is capable of affecting you physically and psychologically. Your literal subconscious ***does not critique data***. You can become convinced of a fact whether it is true or not. Once an idea has been accepted it becomes a reality in your life. This is the case with chronic shame in many people that I have treated with hypnosis. They are told they are dumb or stupid and that becomes their reality until a new set of beliefs is accepted by the subconscious. Hypnosis has clearly demonstrated that when in trance, divination powers of attunement become real for you.

Confidence, belief, self-trust, concentration, and divination are all closely related. Your skill will reflect confidence which is positive, realistic, and active. Your confidence moves in five different directions:

Upward- Towards Divine, Spiritual Confidence
Inward- Towards Personal, Self-Confidence
Outward- Towards Interpersonal, Human Confidence
Forward- Towards Future, Confidence
Backward- Towards Past or Historical Confidence

Each of these directions of our confidence or faith reflect the soul, or our connection to the source. Your subconscious or soul is vibrant, alive and connected. It is goal-oriented and always moving in some direction. That direction can be selected by you, or it can be selected by others. To choose your directions with awareness is exercising your free will. The following points will assist you in gaining mastery of your subconscious resources for divination accuracy.

1. The basic energies are neutral, positive, and negative. These may be seen as neutral, yes, and no. **Ask questions that can be answered with a yes or no response and use the process of elimination to fine-tune your questioning process, by becoming very specific.**

2. It is very important to properly program your subconscious mind to fully grasp and affirm the appropriate responses selected. Once programmed it will respond automatically.

3. It is imperative that you become clear about what you want to know or create. Make your questions and affirmations as simple and clear as possible.

4. Using questions with a time element is also important. Words such as ***currently, past, or future*** will assist you in fine-tuning the most accurate responses. Also, using words such as ***primary or priority*** will prove helpful in defining what you really want to know. Ask yourself, ***"who, what, when and where?"*** Many example questions have been provided to assist you. Words which represent variables, such as name, time, place, or condition, are often <u>underlined</u>.

5. If you find yourself asking ***why me?,*** it is best to move on and ask ***what's next***?

Example Questions: Instead of, ***"Why did John dump me?,"*** ask, What's next! "Is more social interaction in my best interest at this time? More exercise? More study about relationships?"

6. You will notice that many of the example questions are designed in such a way that you can learn to be just as comfortable getting a no, or negative response as a yes or positive one. This will assist you in remaining neutral. I encourage you to form some of your questions this way.

Example Question: Is Fred currently deficient in this vitamin?
If you are Fred, you might see getting a no response to this question as a positive thing! It is important to become comfortable with both aspects of polarity and which ever direction the pendulum swings! Preparing your questions occasionally in this way enhances your being neutrally responsive, not reactive.

7. Your thoughts and feelings emit energy. Many spiritual principles teach us the importance of cause and effect, meaning that we produce our effects as a direct result of our thoughts, feelings, intentions and actions. ***It is important to maintain both mental and emotional neutrality to achieve accuracy. Keep yourself calm and unattached to the responses.*** **Be a witness!** ***See yourself as a neutral part of the pendulum or asking device, rather than as a perceptual person who produces the responses!*** **Go beyond polarity (right / wrong) to a place of absolute neutrality and oneness.**

8. The importance of using samples for diagnosis, such as hair or blood, lists, pictures, illustrations or charts, is emphasized. This will assist you in maintaining mental concentration and emotional neutrality. It is often more effective and easier to point to a written name or illustration and remain neutral than to imagine a person or situation with the same accuracy. This is especially true, if you know the person or see that person's health problem or situation as threatening.

9. It is important to be honest and clear about your intentions. It's as true with the pendulum as it is with any guidance tool that we as seekers must avoid any misuse of the guidance available to us. From a spiritual point of view, the emphasis is on joining our will with God's, or attuning to creative spiritual will. We will explore using our joint creative will for the highest possible good, physically, mentally, and emotionally as we create spiritually and our soul consciousness evolves. If you find that you are not certain of your intention, I suggest that you ask yourself:

- What will I do with this information?
- What action will I take?
- Would this action benefit everyone concerned?
- What action might the person who receives this information take?
- Do I need to question them about their intentions before I help them?

10. Be aware of any vibrational interferences such as loud music, noises, or electronic equipment. My private investigations partner and I compose our questions for psychic or soul location work during the day, and get up at 5 am to do the actual pendulum communications work. The environment is quiet, still and peaceful, and insures our accuracy.

11. Let go of any preconceived ideas! One of my favorite quotes from A Course in Miracles applies here, "The ego does not ask or question, certain that it knows." It is important to put all preconceived notions out of your mind and move beyond your ego to remain neutral and unbiased. You must be a silent, neutral witness!

12. Hindrances to successful divination include: not recognizing trance states as natural, an overly analytical attitude, a "prove it to me" attitude, or trying too hard.

13. It is important to understand that pendulum divination can also be used to go beyond perception to a state of oneness. Pendulum divination can also be used to enhance giving and receiving energy, as well as questioning.

14. It is best to keep your arms and legs uncrossed, with your feet flat on the floor, which keeps your energy meridians uncrossed and functioning optimally.

15. To assist you in remaining neutral, it is best to use your name when asking about yourself, rather than I, me or my. Example questions are presented with various names (underlined) to remind you of this important format. Just insert your own name when asking questions about yourself.

16. It is important to accept that divination transcends both time and space.

17. This is your opportunity to choose Truth, Being, Peace and Oneness first! This aligns you with the vertical, neutral path and out of polarized, horizontal thinking. You can choose to become a wise, centered and neutrally grounded channel of information and blessings. Perhaps making friends with neutrality **and** polarity (duality or paradoxical thinking), with the highest intentions can create miracles. "One should not think slightingly of the paradoxical," said Danish philosopher Soren Kierkegaard, "for the paradox is the source of the thinker's passion, and the thinker without passion is like a lover without a feeling." As Divine Co-creators, each of us participates in using, enhancing and destroying our energies. Co-creation is the honor of Divinity that we must claim for ourselves.

Subconscious Programming for Accurate Divination

— NEGATIVE **Counterclockwise** | **NEUTRAL** **Vertical** | **+ POSITIVE** **Clockwise**

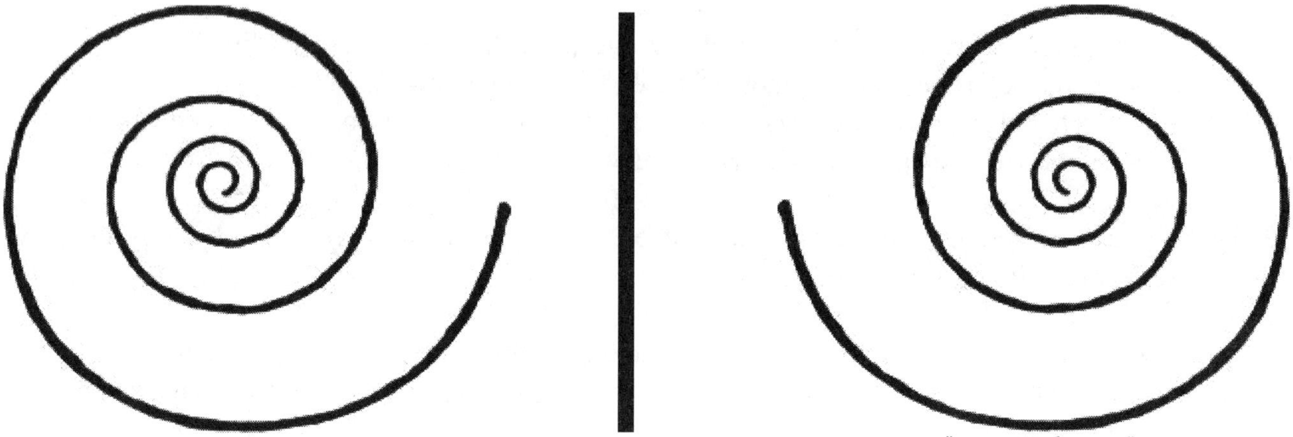

"www.arttoday.com" "www.arttoday.com"

1. Sit comfortably at a table or desk with both your feet flat on the floor. Uncross your arms and legs. Place this diagram in front of you.

2. Close your eyes, breath deeply and take a few moments to relax, calming your mind and emotions. Then, in your own words, reaffirm your intention for the highest good for all concerned in asking for guidance.

3. Open your eyes and hold the pendulum string in your hand between your thumb and forefinger over the vertical line labeled neutral. Allow your eyes to follow the line from the top to the bottom, up and down, up and down. Begin to swing the pendulum up and down, following the vertical line as you say. "This movement indicates neutral energy and neutral response. My subconscious accepts this movement to indicate neutral energy and neutral response."

4. Feel the calm, detached, neutral flow of energy and continue to reaffirm out loud. "This vertical movement indicates neutral energy and neutral response."

5. Hold the pendulum over the clockwise (right-handed) spiral on your right, labeled positive. Allow your eyes to follow this spiral in a clockwise movement, from the center outward, around and around. Swing your pendulum in this clockwise movement and say out loud.,"This movement indicates positive polarity and positive response. Clockwise movement indicates positive polarity and positive, or yes, response."

6. Repeat this several times as you relax and reaffirm the positive or yes response.

7. Hold your pendulum over the counterclockwise (left-handed) spiral on your left, labeled negative. Allow your eyes to follow the spiral in a counterclockwise movement, from the center outward, around and around. Swing your pendulum in this counterclockwise movement and say,
"This movement indicates negative polarity and negative response. Counterclockwise movement indicates negative polarity and negative or no response. "

8. Practice this exercise several times out loud with all three energies, neutral, positive and negative.

9. Now remove the diagram from the table and say out loud. "This movement indicates the neutral energy, neutral response." Then allow and receive the vertical movement and reaffirm it out loud.

10. Then say out loud, "This movement indicates positive energy, positive response." Then allow and receive the clockwise movement and reaffirm it out loud.

11. Then say out loud, "This movement indicates the negative energy, negative response." Then allow and receive the counterclockwise movement and reaffirm it out loud.

12. Practice this exercise every time you begin your questioning sessions until you can get the matching movements and responses easily without using the diagram. This indicates that your subconscious mind is clear about the matching movements and responses.

13. Notice how fast and how wide the circular motion is. As your pendulum swings, estimate on a scale from 1 to 10 how much energy is indicated. The faster and wider the swing, the higher the number. Your response will be recorded as a range extending from 1+ to 10+ (positive) or 1- to 10 - (negative), giving you a large energy scale of 20 total (both positive & negative) points to work with. Small, slow circles are about 1-3 and large fast circles are about 7-10. The direction it spins, tells you if the response is positive or negative (yes or no). You will record answers like this, -4, +9, +2 etc.

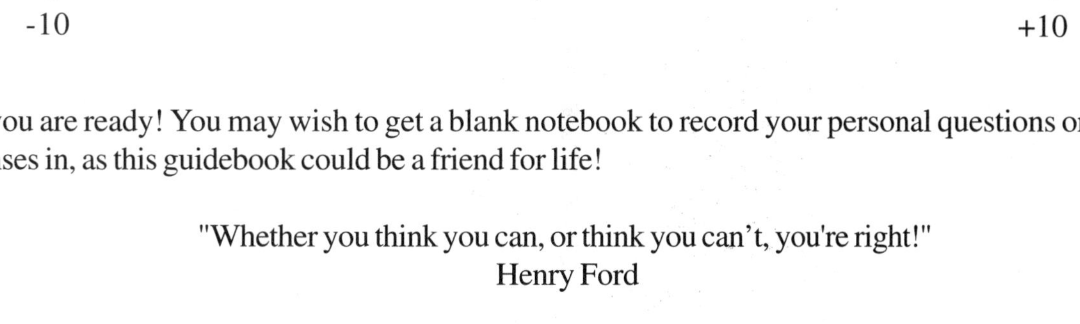

Now you are ready! You may wish to get a blank notebook to record your personal questions or responses in, as this guidebook could be a friend for life!

"Whether you think you can, or think you can't, you're right!"
Henry Ford

Developing Neutrality

The following words will assist you in experiencing true neutrality and serve other advanced applications. Neutrality is the middle way of peace. It is choosing peace first, choosing being, first. Neutrality is the most important aspect of accuracy! Neutrality is where peace and attunement begin.

Relax and center yourself. Hold your pendulum over these words. Allow the neutral/vertical movement and attune to each word as you say them out loud.

neutral
the middle way
witnessing
centered
essence
presence
acceptance
indifference
allowing
compromise
surrender
androgynous
being
highest intentions

Extending Polarities

Polarity is the manifestation of two opposing attributes, tendencies or principles. While it is recommended that you use only neutral, positive and negative to begin with, here is an extended list of polarities which can assist the advanced student. Understanding the mind's infinite ability to adapt, change and create, you can see that using other popular polarities might fit other applications, such as accept / reject for quality control. It is important to maintain congruency with the basic energies of neutral, positive and negative. You will find the following list to be a powerful catalyst for advanced applications. Can you think of other polarities of your own to add to this list?

"www.arttoday.com"

"www.arttoday.com"

counterclockwise	**clockwise**
negative	**positive**
NO	YES
FEMALE	MALE
YIN	YANG
INHARMONIOUS	HARMONIOUS
INCOMPATIBLE	COMPATIBLE
DESTROY	CREATE
REGRESS	PROGRESS
RECEIVE	GIVE
REJECT	ACCEPT
REPEL	ATTRACT
INNER	OUTER
PASSIVE	ACTIVE
STAGNATION	GROWTH
DEFICIENT	SUFFICIENT
UNATTAINABLE	ATTAINABLE
DISLIKE	LIKE
CLOSED	OPEN
FEAR	LOVE

INFERIOR	SUPERIOR
SEPARATE	UNITED
STOP	START
NIGHT	DAY
DARK	LIGHT
LOSE	WIN
CONTRACT	EXPAND
PURGE	REBUILD
INTROVERT	EXTROVERT
YIELDING	FIRM
DEPLETED	FULL
INCOMPLETE	COMPLETE
FORGET	REMEMBER
WEAKNESS	STRENGTH
WANE	WAX
LESS	MORE
REJECTION	ACCEPTANCE
CHRONIC	ACUTE
ABUSE	CORRECT USE
UNCONSCIOUS	CONSCIOUS
RETROGRADE	DIRECT
HARD TO EXPRESS	EASY TO EXPRESS
HARD TO UNDERSTAND	EASY TO UNDERSTAND
INTERNAL	EXTERNAL
LACK OF FAITH	FAITH
SLOW	FAST
OVER OR DONE WITH	IN PROCESS
INTUITIVE	LOGICAL
EXCESS	MODERATION
SPIRITUAL	MUNDANE
SUBJECTIVE	OBJECTIVE
SUBTLE	OBVIOUS
THE OPPOSITE WAY	ONE WAY
INSIDE	OUTSIDE
COVERT, HIDDEN	OVERT OR OBVIOUS
ABSENCE OF, NEED FOR	PRESENCE OF
PROBLEMATIC, STRESSFUL	PROCEEDING SMOOTHLY
PRIVATE	PUBLIC
DELAYED	QUICK
IMAGINED	REAL
UNRELIABLE	TRUSTWORTHY
RESTRICTED	UNINHIBITED
HOLDING BACK	WANTING TO

Exercises For Awakening The Power and Wisdom of Your Soul

"True spiritual and psychological health and growth come only when one stands in the Light of one's own Inner Wisdom, guided and compelled by one's own Soul and the personal plan for one's own life."
Dr. Korra Deaver

These exercises will remind you that, we are all souls infused with Spirit having a multidimensional experience!

"Divination is the creative guesswork of the inquisitive,
evolving soul and oversoul."
Rev. Iris K Barratt

Guess (noun)

(from Roget's 21st Century Thesaurus, Copyright 1996)

Guess, belief, speculation

assumption, ballpark figure*, conclusion, conjecture, deduction, divination, estimate, fancy, feeling, guesstimate*, guesswork, hunch*, hypothesis, induction, inference, judgment, notion, opinion, postulate, postulation, prediction, presumption, presupposition, reckoning, shot*, sneaking suspicion*, stab* supposal, supposition, surmisal, surmise, suspicion, theory, thesis, view

Guess (verb)

to do your best to figure out; imagine

believe, calculate, chance, conjecture, dare say, deduce, deem, divine, estimate, fancy*, fathom, go out on a limb*, guesstimate*, happan upon*, hazard*, hypothesize, infer, judge, jump to conclusion*, lump it*, opine, penetrate, pick, postulate, predicate, predict, presume, pretend, reason, reckon, select, size up*, solve, speculate, suggest, suppose, surmise, survey, suspect, take a shot at*, take a stab at*, theorize, think, think likely, venture, work out*

Oversoul

(from Merriam-Webster Collegiate Dictionary, Copyright 1996)

Oversoul: the absolute reality and basis of all existences concieved as a spiritual being in which the ideal nature imperfectly manifested in human beings is perfectly realized.

Business and Professional

"www.arttoday.com"

Advertising Advantages

What if you could discern which types of advertising would be the most financially rewarding? What if you could discern which advertisements are misleading, according to your own standards?

You can use your pendulum and ask specific questions!

Example Questions:

- Is this advertising true according to Vanessa's standards?
- Would this be a financially rewarding business ad for Vanessa to pursue?
- Would this type of advertising be financially rewarding for my business to pursue for 3 months?

Below are stars used to compare your own possibilities. Using stars in this way automatically lets your mind know that these possibilities are being compared. Write your own advertising possibilities at the edge of each point on a star to compare them. Point to each one with your index finger, while holding the pendulum with your other hand. Become a neutral witness, ask your question and record your response.

Home Buying Considerations

The considerations for home buying are multifaceted. Many of my clients are real estate agents and now use pendulum divination to contribute to their success! Consider the following questions and create your own.

Point to each possibility with your index finger, while holding the pendulum with your other hand. Become a neutral witness, ask your question and record the response.

Example Questions:

- Is it in Lorraine's best interest to accept the current offer on her home?
- Is it in Lorraine's best interest to reject the current offer on her home?
- Would this location have beneficial living factors for Lorraine in the future?
- Would this location have detrimental living factors for Lorraine in the future?
- Would this purchase provide excellent resale advantages for Lorraine in the future?
- Would purchase of this location benefit Lorraine's overall well-being?

Legal Considerations

While the law was created to protect legal rights, some people use it to play attack and defend games. Many people have been victimized by the law when problems caught them unaware, unprepared when they were economically or emotionally disadvantaged. With the rising costs of legal assistance, I encourage you to use your pendulum to ask pertinent questions if you feel your rights have been violated or if you are legally challenged.

Legal questions regarding timing are often of utmost importance, as timing is often a strategy used for manipulation. Consider the following possible questions and create your own as needed.

Point to each possibility with your index finger while holding the pendulum with your other hand. Become a neutral witness, ask your question and record the response.

Example Questions:

- Is it in Tina's best interest to learn more about her legal rights?
- Is it in Tina's best interest to request mediation in this legal matter?
- Is it in Tina's best interest to use a mediator in this legal matter?
- Are Tina's legal rights being abused by her landlord?
- Is it in Tina's best interest to sign this legal document today?
- Is it in Tina's best interest financially to pursue this matter legally?
- Is it in Tina's best interest emotionally to pursue this matter legally?
- Are there more beneficial ways for Tina to pursue this emotional issue?
- Are there other people that this action might damage?
- Is Tina's right to privacy legally being ignored by ABC Collections?
- Is it in Tina's best interest to threaten to pursue this matter legally?
- Are my children at risk emotionally if I take their Mother to court?
- Is it more efficient for Tina to pursue these legal issues in Germany?

Selecting Honorable Employees

Every business owner knows the importance of selecting employees who are trustworthy and honest. Many of the techniques currently used such as lie-detector tests are ineffective. You can use your pendulum to assist in this important selection process.

Point to each possibility with your left index finger, while holding the pendulum with your right hand. Become a neutral witness, ask the question and record the response.

Example Questions:

- Would Don Brown be an asset to our company?
- Is Don Brown reliable?
- Is Don Brown unreliable?
- Is Don Brown trustworthy?
- Is Don Brown dishonest?
- Are Don Brown's intentions honorable?
- Could Don be a highly productive salesman with our company?
- Will employing Don Brown be mutually beneficial for everyone?

Write your questions, using the name of the person in question.

Values Clarification and Risk-taking

This is an exercise that I read somewhere and have enjoyed using for its decision making simplicity. When considering a risk, an action or path of experience, write the following;

List many ***possible positive*** consequences of taking the risk.

List many ***possible negative*** consequences of ***not*** taking the risk.

You may wish to use your pendulum to ask additional questions regarding your lists. Your lists can serve as a catalyst to your questing process!

Do your lists reflect your values?
This is a positive and powerful tool to use with teenagers of any age!

Children

"www.arttoday.com"

Heart Rocks and Loving Attunement

Many of the women and children I love and adore seem to collect heart-shaped rocks.

What if you went to a river bank, a rock pile, or a dirt road with a lot of rocks?
What if you drew a simple picture of a heart-shaped rock and put it in your pocket with the intention of being drawn to and finding heart-shaped rocks?
What if you pretended that your hands were magnetic to heart-shaped rocks?
What if you were naturally drawn to discover several heart rocks in one peace-filled afternoon and had several gifts to share with others? Kids love heart rocks. Some adults with an active inner child appreciate them too. Allow your inner child to trust the attunement process and experience the delightful results.

Hide and Seek

Place a button or small object under one of three plastic drinking glasses.
Turn around and hide your eyes while the children hide the object under the glass that they choose. Use your magic pendulum to find it by asking, "Is the button under this glass?" Keep asking about each cup or glass until the hidden object is found. Share the magic and have childlike fun!

Neutrality Walk

To experience a simple energy connection which may have unlimited healing benefits, go for a neutrality walk.

Walk slowly and swing your arms.

Then begin to relax your arms and begin to feel them as pendulums, swinging fully back and forth and feel the dynamic neutral energy flow through you. Imagine a sense of detachment, as you allow your arms to swing at their own extension and pace.

You may find that saying these positive statements is energizing and beneficial.

I choose the neutral way first.

I choose the middle way first.

I choose to accept peace now.

I choose to accept love now.

Trance Dance

I have always seen and felt the connection between the rhyming words, trance and dance. A trance is defined as "a hypnotic, cataleptic or ecstatic state." Some ancient traditions believe that we are literally in our right minds in trance and that the rational, conscious, everyday level is one of illusion and learning. Some believe the subconscious level is the domain of devils or saints, and the superconsciousness level is where we claim and extend gifts of love, and truth. Each level however, does have its gifts and challenges!

Pendulum questing becomes a form of trance dancing as you attune to and witness the guidance available. We do not need drugs to enter fully into the soul level and evolve with consciousness. We can choose to trance dance in any way that we choose. As you dance the trance of the peacemaker in prayer, meditation or contemplation, you can become a grateful, willing, and observing silent witness. I believe that children can greatly benefit from learning to create a neutral and observing silent witness. What if our children could observe and honor the energies of Spirit and use them with others to witness, receive and give? What are the possible positive consequences of doing our best and what are the possible negative consequences if we don't? As passionate educators and peacemakers we must ask passionate questions. Are you actively co-creating with spiritual willingness and intentions? Do you know and love what you want? Can you create a trance dance to enhance it? The heartfelt love of peace, beauty and harmony does exist in the cosmos and we are all a reflection of that oneness. What if recognizing it and aligning with affirmative action is Divine Intelligence!

Create a Trance Dance for Peace!

I encourage you to create a trance dance for peace with yourself and others. Kids are usually the most fun! I encourage you to speak about the middle way, the observing, silent witness and share a moment of silence with the neutral, vertical pendulum movement. This may be appropriate during a moment of silence when acknowledging a death or illness. Teach children of their inherent right to ask questions and receive and give forth their own inherent grace. You might ask what qualities the group wants to receive and give by reading the spiritual qualities list (page 102). Agree as a group to focus collectively on a chosen quality. Focus your intentions on the quality or essence you wish to receive with the counter clockwise movement and give or send forth a chosen quality with the clockwise or positive movement.

Then have a trance dance to gratefully celebrate life and spiritual well-being.

Trance dancing, fasting, prayer, meditation or contemplation are perhaps the oldest forms of spiritual worship, an ancient passageway into the superconsciousness of Spirit or Divine Love and Intelligence. A familiar awakening into oneness with the oversoul, (spiritual essence or vital force in the universe in which all souls participate, which transcends individual consciousness), the highest level of healing, co-creation and manifestation.

What if only you can do your best! ***What if*** doing your best was even better than you could ever imagine or witness?

30 Common Statements that Children Hear From Adults

From: Donna and Deana Meyer (mother & daughter) in Chula Vista, Calif.

You may find some of these statements very familiar. Negative statements experienced by children at a young age can have very detrimental effects. Point to each possibility with your index finger, while holding the pendulum with your other hand. Become a neutral witness, ask your question and record the response.

Example Questions:

- Has Susan ever had anyone say this to her?
- Was Susan under 16 years old?
- Has Susan ever repeated this to anyone?
- Was Susan ever hurt by this statement?

1. No! (the answer most often heard)
2. Don't give me those excuses!
3. Let me put it another way. . .
4. I don't have time now, maybe later.
5. Do you think I'm made out of money?
6. Just wait till you have kids of your own!
7. What in the world do you think you're doing?
8. Don't eat a snack, dinner's almost ready!
9. Be nice to your little brother (or sister) or else!
10. Clean your room!
11. When I was your age. . .
12. Are you lying to me?
13. Eat your dinner, there are children starving all over the world!
14. Can't you understand what I'm trying to tell you!
15. Can't you ever do (or get) anything right?
16. Who do you think you are anyway?
17. Why don't you grow up?
18. This is going to hurt me more than it hurts you!
19. When are you ever going to learn?
20. Do it now!
21. Can't you kids get along with each other?
22. Why can't you be like __________?
23. Go to your room!
24. Do your homework!
25. Don't use that tone of voice with me!
26. Shut up and listen!
27. You're not old enough to understand that yet!
28. Here, let me show you how to do it right!
29. I'm doing this for your own good!
30. Turn that radio down (off)!

Uncommon Things Adults Enjoy Saying to Children

Do any of these statements sound familiar to you? Positive statements expressed to children when they are young can help them to have a more positive outlook about life and themselves. Point to each possibility with your index finger while holding the pendulum with your other hand. Become a neutral witness, ask your question and record the response.

Example Question:

•Would my children (or this child) benefit from this response?

Ask yourself: What do I want to ask? What do I want to know? What do I want to say? How do I want to say it?

1. Yes, please.
2. Please share with me what happened.
3. Let me do my best to make it clearer for you.
4. I'd like to pursue that together right after dinner!
5. I'll do my best to assist you in creating that opportunity.
6. Someday I hope you will deepen your learning through children.
7. What in the Universe are you creating now?
8. Dinner is almost ready, do you wish to wait?
9. I think we're all happiest when the two of you show love and respect for each other! Let's do our best and start again.
10. Would you please clean your room by this Sunday?
11. It is interesting for me to remember when I was your age!
12. Are you telling the truth in the best way you can?
13. If you don't eat all your dinner, please be sure that it doesn't go to waste.
14. I'm not sure that I'm doing my best to help you understand me.
15. I love watching you get it right so quickly, you're such a fast learner!
16. Are you feeling confused about who you are right now?
17. I will do my best to assist your maturing process.
18. I feel sad and angry when I feel like punishing you. I want so much good for you, I encourage you to create better options for yourself.
19. It inspires me to watch you learn and grow!
20. Can you please help me now?
21. Can you children choose to get along and love each other more now?
22. It is beneficial to look beyond comparison with people and appreciate their uniqueness!

Education and Research

"www.arttoday.com"

Educational and Research Applications

Finding books and information which apply to your specific needs is certainly a challenge! Finding the educational subjects, schools, or teachers, that will benefit you most, can change your life! You can enhance your lifelong learning by actively locating and participating in your areas of interest. Hold the pendulum over your list or book and ask your questions.

Example Question:

- Is the information in this book currently beneficial to Linda's research?
- Is UCLA the best school for Linda's education in economics?
- Does this chapter have applicable legal information on animal rights?
- Does this book have the information Linda is seeking on transpersonal therapy?
- Does this file have the information on Linda's leasing agreement?

Write your own questions, go to the library or the Internet and get your lists or illustrations.

Choosing a Hobby or Career

You can use your pendulum to discover natural abilities for rewarding hobbies, activities or occupations for yourself or loved ones.

Point to each activity with your index finger, while holding the pendlum with your other hand. Become a neutral witness, ask your question and record your response. Remember to use your name when asking about yourself.

Example Questions:

- Could this be a financially rewarding activity for Paul?
- Could this be a financially rewarding activity for Paul in Utah?
- Is this activity aligned with Paul's natural abilitites?
- Could this be a personally rewarding hobby for Paul?
- Could this be a personally rewarding activity for our Seniors Center?

Fashion Designer
Tour Guide
Song Writer
Wedding Planner
Party Planner
Movie Critic
Portrait Photographer
Computer Programmer
Actress/Actor
Restaurant Owner
House Sitter
Animal Groomer
Secretary
Hotel Owner
Politician
Real Estate Agent
Insurance Agent
Banking
Dentist
Management
Physician
Detective
Painting
Animal Nurturing
Musical instrument
Singing

Fund-raiser
Import/Export
College Professor
Interior Designer
Chef
Journalist
Bus Driver
Pilot
Bank Teller
Clothing Store Owner
Animal Sitter
Office Assistant
Painter
Carpenter
Florist
Engineer
Pharmacist
Health Care
Inventor
Musician
Geologist
Forester
Astrology
Aerobics
Dancing
Gardening

Herbalist
Novelist
Teacher
Event Planner
Chauffeur
Nature Photographer
Clown
Flight Attendant
Waitress/ Waiter
Shop Keeper
Dog Walker
Business Person
Maid
Farmer
Nurse
Economist
Hairdresser
Stock Broker
Sales
Veterinarian
Advertising
Funeral Director
Collecting
Tutoring
Mentoring
Child Care

Multiple Intelligence Skills and Education
adapted from Linda Gardner's Workshop on
Teaching and Learning through Multiple Intelligences, 1992

By integrating a broader understanding of what constitutes "intelligence," parents and educators can enhance the success of each child's learning ability. Helping each individual find his or her best ways of learning and focusing on building those strengths is a critical part of creating a "learning" mentality. Exposing every child to the following range of intelligences can assist them in developing broader ways of thinking.

The belief that there are multiple ways of being "smart" helps encourage the acceptance and development of a more diverse society. For example, accepting Michael Jordans athletic genuis (bodily/kinesthetic) as just as genuine as Einstein's logical/mathmatical genius. Point to each of these intelligence areas and ask the following questions:

Example Questions:

- Is Michael currently expressing this intelligence quality?
- Is Michael currently deficient in this intelligence quality?
- Is it in Michael's best interest to focus on developing this intelligence quality now?

Point your finger to each intelligence quality and ask your question.

Bodily/ Kinesthetic

Verbal/Linguistic

Musical/Rhythmic

Logical/Mathematical

Visual/Spatial

Intrapersonal

Interpersonal

Naturalist

Family and Relationships

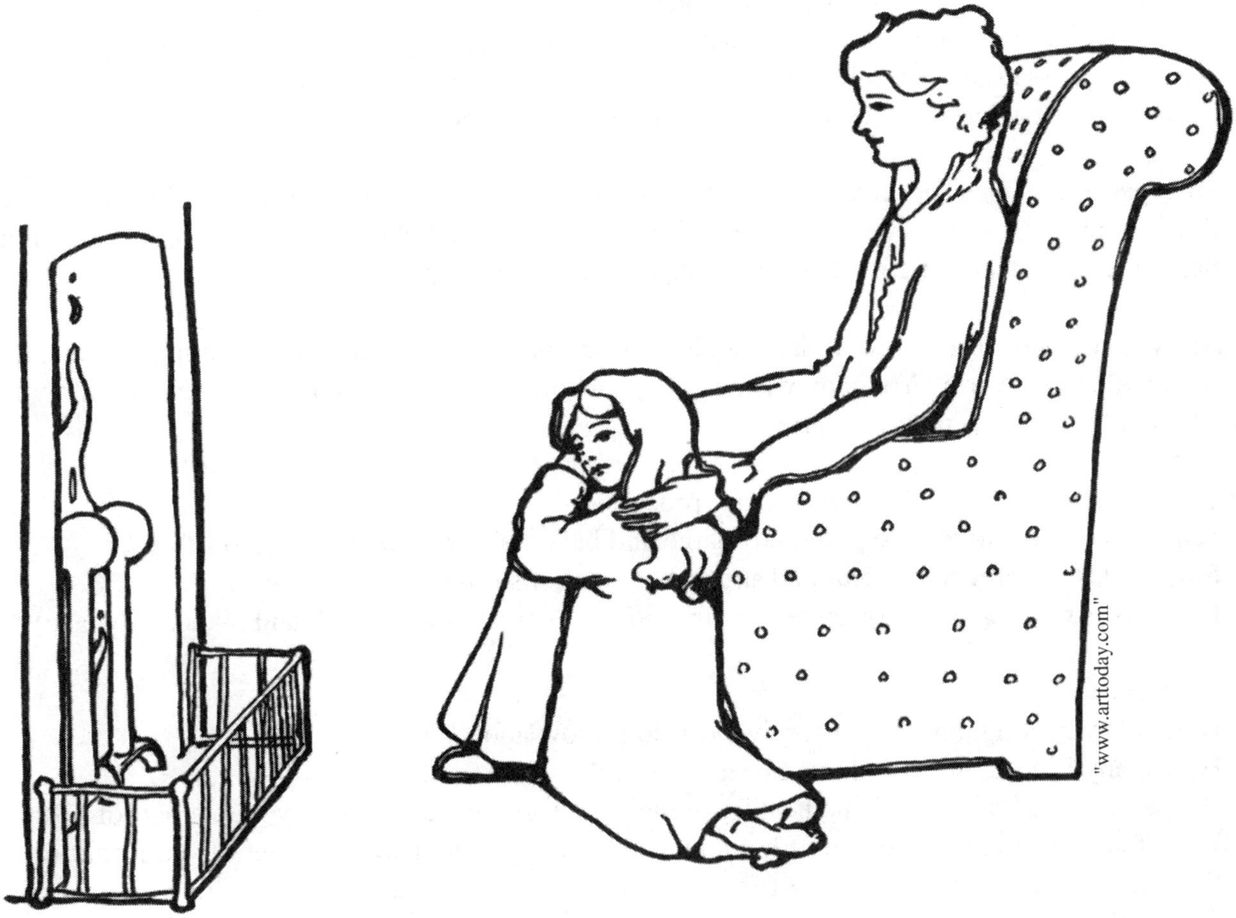

Creating Miracles of Forgiveness

Many great religions and spiritual beings have emphasized the importance of forgiveness and returning to love. However, we are not always taught how to forgive. Many forgiveness experts agree that we would forgive more if we knew how. To experience the true benefits of forgiveness involves doing the inner work necessary to release negativity on all levels, physical, mental, emotional and spiritual.

Forgiveness does not mean that we condone or agree with the actions of others. It is sometimes best not to tell offenders about our choice and process to forgive, to avoid revictimization. To forgive requires willingness to hold a positive attitude for your health and well-being. It is a life-affirming process which allows you to release fear, doubt, anger, resentment, disharmony, and move forward.

To experience peace and love, first create emotional freedom through forgiveness. Forgiveness requires a commitment to take responsibility for your choices and allow others to take responsibility for theirs. See the order blank for self-hypnosis tapes on forgiveness processes.

Are you ready to accept that we have a global responsibility to create more healing, peace and freedom within our world? You may wish to ask yourself, "Is what I am currently creating in my life what I want to take with me into eternity?"

Forgiveness often includes these three inner processes:

Self forgiveness (to release guilt and shame and become more self-compassionate.)
Forgiveness of others (to clear and strengthen relationships)
Forgiveness of a group, organization, or Nation (to create more local, and planetary peace)

Ask yourself:

- How many healing miracles of forgiveness do I know about?
- How many healing miracles have I been a part of?
- How aware am I of the fact that healing miracles of forgiveness are a very viable part of history?
- What feelings or experiences am I holding against myself that I would benefit from forgiving?
- Who are the people in my life that I feel have mistreated me, that I would benefit from forgiving?
- Am I willing to move forward for my own health and well-being as well as effect the bigger picture of love in my life and the lives of others?
- What groups in my life have treated me or others unfairly, that I would benefit from forgiving? Governmental agencies? Judicial systems? Some military? A specific race, culture or Nation? A specific Religious group? A business group?
- Am I willing to do the inner work, gain clarity and allow myself to release on all levels and return to love?
- Have I considered what the alternatives might looks like?

You can recieve grace with a counterclockwise pendulum movement and send it back out with a positive statement, using the clockwise pendulum movement and be a part of the solution.

Family History

There are often unknown elements regarding family history which are meaningful to explore. Adopted children may wish to ask questions regarding hereditary tendencies when making medical decisions. Tracing personal or hereditary information regarding ancestors is another great way to use your pendulum divination skills. Many people trace geneology with the intention of forgiving and healing past patters within their families. You may wish to ask questions regarding hereditary illnesses or family characteristics which you desire to change. You may wish to gather information from family members regarding hereditary tendencies. Consider the following questions and then create your own.

Point to each possibility with your index finger, while holding the pendulum with your other hand. Become a neutral witness, ask your question and record the response.

Example Questions:

- Does heart disease run in Oliver's family on his biological father's side?
- Is arthritis a hereditary tendency in Oliver's family?
- Is depression a hereditary tendency in Oliver's family?
- Was Oliver's grandfather born in Frankfurt, Germany?
- Are there other heirs to Oliver's grandfather's estate?
- Was Oliver's great grandmother part Swiss?
- Was Oliver's great grandmother a Christian?
- Was Oliver related to Julie in a past life?
- Was Julie a father to Oliver in a past life?

Harmonious Relationships and Compatibility

Relationships play a big part in our lives, as they influence every area of our lives individually and collectively. You can use your pendulum to discover harmonious or inharmonious aspects within any relationship by observing the direction, strength and size of the circular movement. Write your name as name #1 when asking about yourself. Point to names 1 and 2 with your index finger, while holding the pendulum with your other hand. Become a neutral witness, ask your question and record the response.

Example Questions:

- Are these people generally compatible?
- Are these people physically compatible?
- Are these people mentally compatible?
- Are these people emotionally compatible?
- Are these people spiritually compatible?
- Are these people socially compatible?
- Are these people financially compatible?

You may wish to fine-tune your questions, such as:

- Are these people compatible for deep intimacy?
- Are these people sexually compatible?
- Would these people be compatible partners as parents?
- Do these people have similar parenting styles?
- Are these people domestically compatible?
- Are these people religiously compatible?
- Are these people geographically compatible?
- Are these people genetically compatible?
- Would these people be compatible travel partners?
- Is it in Susan's best interest to pursue a long term friendship with Ronda?
- Is there a deep loving soul connection between Melissa and trees?
- Has Ronda ever been in a past life relationship with Pat?

Name #1 Name #2

I have found it very important to focus and build on the compatible or harmonious levels with loved ones and family members. You can do this by writing affirmations.

"An affirmation is more than just words that are spoken. An affirmation is a belief, a dedication. It is a powerful statement of personal understanding." Wilferd Peterson, The Art of Creative Thinking.

Write your own affirmative statements and imagine the loved one as you send your affirmations forth with the clockwise pendulum movement.

Example Affirmations:

- I, Iris am grateful to recognize and enhance my emotional compatibility with my daughter Lissa.
- I, Iris am grateful to recognize and enhance all emotionally compatible activities and responses expressed by my daughter Lissa.
- I am grateful to recognize that there a deep loving soul connection between myself, Iris and my children, Lissa and Leah.
- I am grateful to recognize that there a deep loving soul connection between Leah and her animal friends and trees.

Love Letter Technique

This technique for emotional clarity and release has been published by many relationship experts in many different books. As a therapist, I have found this technique to be a very powerful communication tool because it:

assists you to create emotional clarity on every level
assists you to experience emotional expression and release
assists you to rationally accept feelings as irrational or exaggerated
assists you to tell the whole truth to yourself and others in a fair and honest manner, which is where true healing occurs

You may use choose to write a love letter just for yourself.

You may use choose to write a love letter to another person keeping your letter and send that person this outline, asking them to participate in the process by writing one to you. You may then choose to exchange letters. This helps each one to tell the whole truth to oneself and others, and makes each person feel fully heard.

You may choose to then each read the other person's letter to back to them. Speaking each other's true feelings on every level of emotion and hearing them in this way, has unlimited healing power. We all need to be heard and to courageously hear others. We all need to tell our own emotional truth.

CONFLICT RESOLUTION: express how you feel on every level (tell the whole truth), ask for what you want, ask the other person to do the same, find the common ground, practice forgiveness as necessary and move forward into greater resolution and healing. Insert your name and use your pendulum to ask questions regarding these levels of emotion and people or situations in your life.

Example Questions:

- Has Jake fully expressed and cleared this level of emotion?
- Has Jake fully expressed and cleared this level of emotion with Tom?
- Is it in Jake's best interest to write this letter to Tom and send it?

LOVE LETTER FORMAT

Here is a summary of each section of the love letter. Begin by filling in the blanks and expressing your anger, resentment, and blame and allow yourself to move through the other emotional levels until you get down to the love. The following lead-in phrases will help you to move on if you get stuck at one level.

1. Anger and Blame

   I hate it when. . .

   It makes me furious when. . .

   I'm fed up with. . .

   I'm tired of. . .

   I resent. . .

2. Hurt and Sadness

   It hurts me when. . .

   I feel sad when. . .

   I feel awful because. . .

   I'm disappointed that. . .

3. Hurt and Insecurity

   I'm afraid that. . .

   I feel scared that. . .

   I am worried that. . .

4. Remorse and Responsibility

   I'm sorry that . . .

   I'm sorry for. . .

   Please forgive me for. . .

   I didn't mean to. . .

5. Intention and wishes

   I want. . .

   I wish. . .

   I hope. . .

6. Understanding, Gratitude, Love, Forgiveness,

   I understand that. . .

   Thank you for. . .

   I love you because. . .

   I'm proud of you for. . .

"www.arttoday.com"

Pet Smart

Although it is wise to consult animal medical professionals when your pets are ill, you can often point your veterinarian in the right direction or get a second opinion with pendulum communications. You can choose to play a more active role in the health and wellness of your pets by assisting in their diagnosis, treatments and healing processes.

Medical insight by scanning the body

Use your pendulum to ask specific questions regarding any part or system of the body. You can do this in either of these two ways:

1. Touch the body in question with one hand and observe the pendulum with your other hand.
2. Use a map or picture of the body part or body system. A copy of ***any*** veterinary medical book with good illustrations can be used. This is especially helpful because the information desired is related to a being who is often difficult to communicate with or if you do not know the names of the body parts in question. Our minds are so aware, we don't need to know the technical name for the body part. Pointing to an illustration will work. Diagnosing in this non-invasive and totally humane way works with pets and animals of every sort.

Dowsing procedure for medical insight of animals

Touch the actual body part or a picture of it, with one hand, while using the pendulum with your other hand.

Example Questions:

- Is this the part of my cat's body which is causing her pain?
- Is this leg broken?
- Is this ankle sprained?
- Does this dog have distemper?
- Does this dog have rabies?
- Has this animal been poisoned?
- Was this animal poisoned intentionally?
- Is this animal pregnant?
- Are Snuggle's unborn babies purebred?
- Is this baby kitten a female?
- Are May 3-6 the most fertile days for breeding my mare?

Fine-tune by using a list of possible conditions.

- Are Spot's kidneys infected?
- Are Spot's kidneys swollen?
- Are Spot's kidneys toxic?
- Is Spot's left kidney punctured?

Travel & Personal Safety

Here are some questions regarding safe travel and personal safety. Use them as a catalyst and then create your own questions as needed.

Point to each possibility with your index finger while holding the pendulum with your other hand. Become a neutral witness, ask your question and record the response.

Example Questions:

- Is this car safe for Teresa to drive to Idaho?
- Is this airplane safe for travel to England?
- Is it safe to continue driving in this snow storm?
- Will bad weather effect the safety of our trip to London?
- Did Teresa lock her door?
- Is Highway 21 safe for travel tonight in a four wheel drive car?
- Will the children continue to sleep while I go to the store for medication?
- Are the children in apartment C alone?
- Are the children in apartment C safe?
- Do the children in apartment C have something contagious?
- Will flight #627 arrive on time in Denver?
- Will it be safe for Teresa to travel alone in Greece during April?

"Being the best expert on you,
your choices, and every facet
of your life is a
sacred responsibility."

Rev. Iris K. Barratt

Health and Wellness

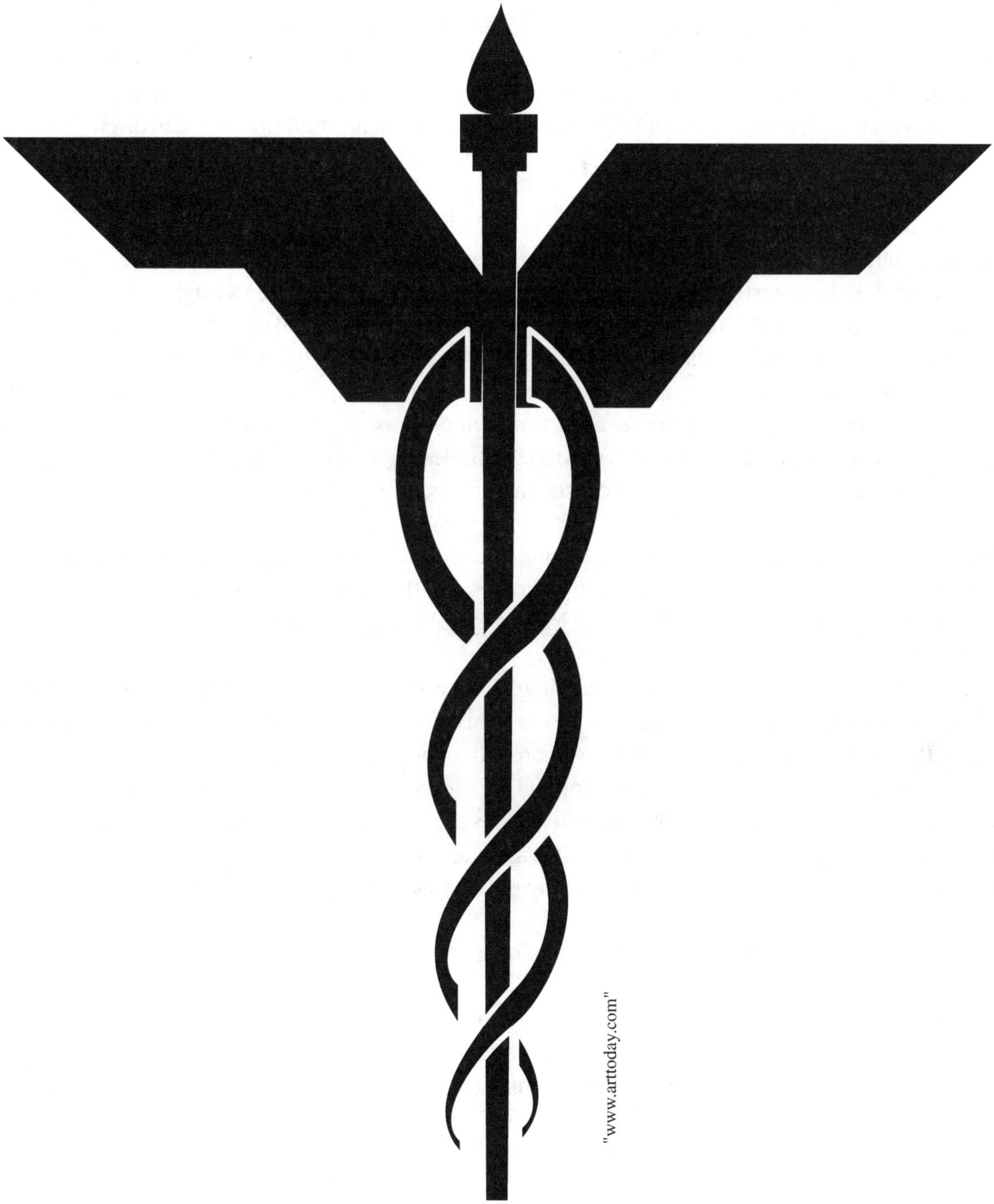

Health and Wellness

Today, with the increasing use of more natural and alternative methods of healing and the rising costs of health care, pendulum divination is a priceless tool! Perhaps the most powerful aspect of these exercises is the opportunity they create for you to actively participate in your own personal diagnosis, treatment and wellness choices. Many new thought medical practitioners, like Dr. Bernie Seigel, emphasize the vital importance of participating in your own healing process, as all healing is ultimately self-healing. Only you can evolve and manifest your power for healing. You are responsible for the health care choices you make. Although it is wise to consult medical professionals in serious medical situations, you can often point them in the right direction or get a second opinion with pendulum divination.

A common practice is to use a sample or witness, which refers to a lock of hair, fingernail, spot of blood, urine or saliva as a personal point of reference. This sample or witness, is a specimen of some part of the person for which the investigation or questions are focused. For example, a sample may be used to help discern an illness, level of health in a specific organ or appropriate medicinal dosages. This sample can be placed in a hollow pendulum. This is similar to using a person's name, picture or illustration to assist the divination process. I believe these samples or symbols like the pendulum or dowsing rod, are simply external objects which serve to awaken or signal a discernment process which transcends time and space. I believe there is no power in these external symbols or samples beyond the facilitation of belief or possible attunement to whatever accounts for the processes and discoveries of divination.

Radionics has the potential to transform allopathic medicine, as well as natural forms of healing. For further information on the theory and practice of radionics, I highly recommend David V. Tansley's excellent book entitled, <u>Radionics, Science or Magic, A Holistic Paradigm of Radionic Theory and Practice</u>. Mr. Tansley states:

"Every healing art functions in relationship to a frame of reference, be it physical, psychological, emotional, spiritual or a combination of two or three of those elements. These frameworks reflect the belief systems upon which the healing art in question bases its approach to the diagnosis and treatment of disease. If that framework is predominantly physical it may promote suppressive or invasive techniques of healing such as drugs or surgery. If it is spiritual then the physical aspects are not given that much importance and as a result, treatment is of a more gentle and subtle nature. It is a matter of observation that the wider frames of reference generally have no difficulty in accommodating the narrower ones, but the reverse is seldom true.

Spiritual healers, for example, have no problem integrating the psychological and physical aspects of patients into their belief system, they are as evident as the spiritual. Medicine on the other hand, being predominately physically based, cannot easily accommodate the spiritual aspects. It had trouble enough integrating the psychological approach to health in the early years of this century, and even today frequently treat mental illness with suppressive drugs where counseling or visualization may well be a better treatment choice."

While many healing experts agree about the powers of the "mind over matter" and that imagination, therapeutic imagery and prayer are the keys to healing, let us remember that all of these tools are faculties of the soul. I believe the soul includes the higher powers of the mind, emotions, intentions and will.

In healing, I see the importance of moving beyond our separate, horizontal, polarized perceptions of judgement and comparison (see page 27-28), into neutrality, oneness, and acceptance. Do you remember sign language for, "you drive me crazy?" Do you remember twirling your fingers around your ears at the end for crazy? That represents crazy, horizontal thinking or being caught up in duality or polarity. Polarity, (polarized thinking), can be a valuable tool and ally or the basis of illusion. The causes and effects of polarized, horizontal thinking (either/or thinking) can lie at the heart of illusion and destruction. How do we move beyond our horizontal, polarized perceptions in a fear based world of comparison and illusion?
It is when we start from the center, vertical path of oneness and acceptance that we manifest the most beneficial causes and effects in healing and all other co-creation. We can find the inner resources of life, love and truth within neutrality ***and*** polarity, enabeling us to use our powers of discernment constructively

It is my hope that given the information and exercises that follow, you will choose to play a more active role in your health and wellness by actively assisting in your diagnosis, treatments and healing processes. **You can also use your intuition to write down and question a list of possible causes of your illnesses.** There are literally hundreds of factors that effect our vulnerability to illness such as heredity, our environment and our attitudes. Many people believe that the predominant factors for health and happiness or sickness and misery are within our own control. Seeking information (divination), using the pendulum as a symbolic means of communication, has honestly served me in countless situations to accurately assist each of these situations. You may wish to refer to page 71 for information relating to environment and attitudes. If you were to make lists of possible causes for health and possible causes for illness, what would you put on them?

Allergies

Many people suffer from allergies and the numbers are growing. Allergies are said to be caused by an immune system that is overprotective towards the body. Some allergy testing has been very unpleasant. Common allergy symptoms include sneezing, runny nose, itchy eyes or lack of energy.
You can use your pendulum to ask questions regarding possible allergies relating to yourself or others.

Point to each possibility with your index finger, while holding the pendulum with your other hand. Become a neutral witness, ask your question and record the response.

Example Questions:

- Is this allergy currently a problem for Amy?
- Has this allergy been a problem for Amy in the past?

Write your questions below, using the name of the person in question.

Food
Alcohol
Drug
Animal
Bacteria
Skin
Metals
Cosmetics
Bees
Bites and stings
Plants
Cigarettes
Feathers
Fibers
Wool
Pollutants
Grasses
Insect products
Insulin

Pollens
Grasses & grass like plants
Trees & shrubs
Weeds & herbs
Medications
(Continue to ask more specific questions if needed.)

Write your own questions to fine-tune for more specific allergens.

Addictions

The American Heritage Dictionary defines addicted as, "Devoting or giving oneself habitually or compulsively." This exercise can be helpful if you suspect that you, a friend or loved one might be challenged by addiction. Insert the name of the person in question, point to each possibility with your index finger, while holding the pendulum with your other hand. Become a neutral witness, ask your question and record the response.

Example Questions:

- Is Donald's habitual soap opera watching a potential addiction?
- Is this the greatest addiction facing our neighborhood teens?
- Is this addiction a current problem for Donald's parents?
- Has this addiction been a problem for Donald in the past?

control	perfectionism	work	drama	illness
worry	deceit	alcohol	drugs	sex
television	Internet	people	food	tobacco
religion	thrill seeking	sleep	money	exercise

Can you think of other possible addictions?

"www.arttoday.com"

Arthritis and Treatments

Arthritis affects millions of people. Do you suffer from the ravages of arthritis? If so, the following questions may prove beneficial.

Insert the proper name of the person in question, point to each possibility with your index finger, while holding the pendulum with your other hand. Become a neutral witness, ask your question and record the response.

Example Questions:

- Is this the type of arthritis _______________ is currently experiencing?
  (name)
- Is _________________ currently experiencing this type of arthritis?
  (name)

You may wish to consult a medical text for a more comprehensive list of arthritis types and treatments. The following lists represent the most common types and treatments.

Rheumatoid Arthritis
Polymyalgia
Raynauds Pheumatica
Reiter's Syndrome
Sjogren's Syndrome
Osteoarthritis
Systematic Lupis Erthematosus
Scleroderma
Gout
Juvenile Arthritis
Lupus

Possible Arthritis Treatments

Point to each possibility with your index finger, while holding the pendulum with your other hand. Become a neutral witness, ask your question and record the response.

Example Question:

- Is this currently the best type of treatment for Grandma's arthritis?

Write your questions, using the name of the person in question.

Possible Arthritis Treatments

Aspirin
Nonsteroidal anti-inflammatory drugs
Corticosteroid drugs
Gold treatments
Penecillamine
Acupuncture
Immunosupressive drugs
Diet
Exercise
Hot and cold treatments
Color therapy
Cell salts
Amino acids
Surgery
Herbs
Essential oils

To get even more specific, you might use the example lists below to discern the best type and duration for exercise. You could also add your own exercise possibilities.

Example Questions:

- Is this currently the best type of exercise for Grandma's arthritis?

  walking
  swimming
  bicycling
  yoga

- How many hours is optimal for Grandma to swim each day?

  1 2 3 4 5 6 7

- How many days per week is optimal for Grandma to swim?

  1 2 3 4 5 6 7

Cell Salts (Biochemical Tissue Remedies)

Cell salts are constituents of various parts of the body. Some are binders, some builders, and others facilitate elimination. They work together to assist in maintaining the electrochemical balance in the body, as well as to balance acidity and alkalinity. These salts come in various potencies from 1X to 12X. The higher the number, the higher the potency, or frequency. These tissue salts are directly assimilated into the blood stream and act immediately. They are dissolved under the tongue three to four times daily. They are sometimes used as a natural antidepressant. (see resources, page 113)

Point to each possibility with your index finger, while holding the pendulum with your other hand. Become a neutral witness, ask your question and record your response.

Example Questions:

- Is Steven currently deficient in this cell salt?
- Would Steven currently benefit from taking this cell salt for indigestion?
- Would Steven currently benefit from taking bioplasma for health maintenance?

calcium fluoride

calcium phosphate

calcium sulphur

ferrum phosphate or phosphate of iron

kali muriaticum or potassium chloride

kali phosphoricum or potassium phosphate

kali sulphuricum or potassium sulphate

magesium phosphuricum or magnesium phosphate

natrum muriaticum or sodium phosphate

natrum sulphuricum or sodium sulphate

silcea or silicic oxide

bioplasma (combination cell salt remedy)

Dosages

Often our bodies vary in their needs for medications or herbal remedies. Divining for dosages is extremely valuable, especially when working with elders who can't remember if they took their medication.

Example Questions:

- Is this the best amount for Steven to take three times daily?
- Has Gladys already taken all her medications today?

Chakra Balancing, Color Breathing and Toning

Our energy units, or chakra movements, are naturally discernible with a pendulum. You can breath in color and sound or hum the musical note for each. Some believe that by blessing each chakra in this way, you can revitalize it. You can discern the energy of each chakra vortex most easily by holding your pendulum above someone lying down on their back.

Hold the pendulum over the 1st chakra and it will naturally move clockwise or counterclockwise, notice the direction and wideness of energy movement, merely observe and record each answer. You may ask the person to imagine the color associated with the chakra and reaffirm the qualities associated with each.

You may ask to enhance the energy as you visualize the same color and sound the same note in your mind or out-loud. You may also imagine sending healing energy to each chakra. See resource listings on page 113 to gain more understanding of chakras.

Chakra	Area of influence	Color	Musical Note
1. Coccygeal	Grounding and Earth Connection	red	C
2. Reproductive	Emotional and Sexual Response	orange	D
3. Solar Plexus	Personal Power and Initiative	yellow	F
4. Heart	Love, Trust and Life Affirming	green	G
5. Throat	Communication and Expression	blue	B
6. Third Eye	Intuition and Spiritual Magnetism	indigo	A
7. Crown	Advanced Spiritual Development	violet	E

Common Types of Cancer

Everyone knows that early cancer detection is vital. Cancer is now second to heart and circulatory diseases as a cause of death in the United States. Virtually all tissues and organs are susceptible. You may wish to use your intuition and ask questions regarding the possible causes of this illness. Some people might question if their illness is caused by past life or hereditary tendencies or maybe emotional or psychological factors. Please celebrate your health with this exercise and research further information when necessary.

Point to each possibility with your index finger, while holding the pendulum with your other hand. Become a neutral witness, ask your question and record the response.

Common Types of Cancer

1. Endometrium
2. Breast
3. Cervical
4. Prostate
5. Bladder
6. Colon
7. Rectum
8. Stomach
9. Lung
10. Pancreas
11. Lymphatic

Example Questions:

- Is Ryan's body currently free of this cancer?
- Is Ryan's body currently experiencing this cancer?
- Is this type of cancer slow to spread?

Exploring Therapeutic Treatments

Below is a list of therapeutic treatment possibilities. For a more comprehensive list, I recommend Barbara Nash's excellent book, From Acupressure to Zen, An Encyclopedia of Natural Therapies. Point to each possibility with your index finger, while holding the pendulum with your other hand. Become a neutral witness, ask your question and record the response.

Example Question:

•Is this currently the best type of treatment for Terri's current problem?

Treatment Modalities:

Psychotherapy	Hypnotherapy	Regression Therapy
Progression Therapy	Desensitization	Medication
EMDR	Voice Dialogue	Therapeutic Imagery
Color Therapy	Sounds & Music	Acupuncture
Acupressure	Biofeedback	Ayurveda
Homeopathic Medicine	Naturopathic Medicine	Art Therapy
Guided Imagery	Yoga	Meditation
Holotropic Breathwork	Aromatherapy	Massage Therapy
Chiropractic Medicine	Feldenkrais Method	Group Therapy
Rolfing	Nutrition	Fasting
Cell Salts	Bach Flowers	Herbalism
Trager Method	Relaxation	Medical Astrology
Shamanism	Tibetan Medicine	Oriental Medicine
Kinesiology	Iridology	Music

Add your own therapy possibilities or questions.

Fears and Phobias

Here is a list of common phobias. You may find it interesting to ask about yourself in relation to each. Point to each possibility with your index finger, while holding the pendulum with your other hand. Become a neutral witness, ask your question and record the response.

Example Questions:

- Does Terri have an inherent tendency towards this fear?
- Is this fear (phobia) currently a problem for Terri?
- Has this fear been a problem for Terri in the past?

Write your questions, using the name of the person in question.

Acrophobia	Height
Agora-	Open spaces
Ailuro-	Cats
Archno-	Spiders
Antho-	Flowers
Anthropo-	People
Agua-	Water
Astra-	Lightning
Bronto-	Thunder
Claustro-	Closed Spaces
Cyno-	Dogs
Demento-	Insanity
Equino-	Horses
Herpeto-	Lizards, Reptiles
Mikro-	Germs
Muro-	Mice
Myso-	Dirt, Uncleanliness
Numero-	Numbers
Nycto-	Darkness
Ophido-	Snakes
Pyso-	Fire
Thanato-	Death
Tricho-	Hair
Xeno-	Stranger
Zoo-	Animal

Holodynamics

From Holodynamics by V. Woolf PH.D, Harbinger House

The following chart shows the six stages of development, referred to as “The Implicate Order." The universe is considered holodynamic by some of the most advanced minds of our time. This means that all matter, energy and intelligence-past, present, and future-are part of one dynamic whole and have an underlying enfolded order. It is called the Implicate Order and the mind, holodynes (sub-personalities), human beings and all of manifest reality follow these same six stages of development. The Implicate Order governs everything living and nonliving, from the smallest cells to subatomic particles to human societies and the universe itself. For further information on these facinating subjects, please refer to the appendix on page 112.

Point to each possibility on the chart, with your index finger, while holding the pendulum with your other hand. Become a neutral witness, ask your question and record the response.
Example questions are listed on the following page.

I	II	III	IV	V	VI
Physical Well-being	Personal Well-being	Interpersonal Well-being	Social Well-being	Principled Well-being	Universal Well-being
Vitality Abundance Health Strength Energy ***To Live*** ***CHOOSE*** ***Not*** ***To Live*** Deprivation "Dingbat" role Dis-ease Zero Power Shut Down	Creativity Confidence Self-assertion "I am OK" Self-discovery ***To Unfold*** ***CHOOSE*** ***Not*** ***To Unfold*** Denial Fear Anger Insecurity Self-defeating	Intimacy Friendship "We are OK" Mutual respect Rapport ***To Commit*** ***CHOOSE*** ***Not*** ***To Commit*** Disconnected Manipulator "Match my images" Pleaser Victim	Synergy Teamwork Open Trust Comradery Cooperation ***To Act*** ***CHOOSE*** ***Not*** ***To Act*** Conformist "Shoulds" Rule-bound Role-bound Judger	Integrity "I am" Owning It fair care share Openness ***To Become*** ***CHOOSE*** ***Not*** ***To Become*** Rationalizer Pretentious Hypocrite Unethical Unscrupulous	Oneness Knowing Empowered Loving Attuned ***To extend*** ***CHOOSE*** ***Not*** ***To Extend*** Detached Remote Aggrandized Obsessed Tyrannical
Physical Disorder	Personal Disorder	Interpersonal Disorder	Social Disorder	Principled Disorder	Universal Disorder

Holodynamics (continued)

Insert your name and ask the following questions.

Example Questions:

- Is Jeanie currently choosing physical well-being?
- Is Jeanie currently choosing personal well-being?
- Is Jeanie currentlychoosing interpersonal well-being?
- Is Jeanie currently choosing social well-being?
- Is Jeanie currently choosing principled well-being?
- Is Jeanie currently choosing universal well-being?
- Is Jeanie currently choosing any other word on the chart?
- Is this level Jeanie's most important current focus?
- Is this level Jeanie's most important karmic path to serve right now?
- Does this level inherently reflect Jeanie's most important skills and natural talents?
- Is Jeanie currently stuck on this level?

Laws for Health and Well-being

adapted from unknown author

How do you choose to sustain your health and well-being? As you read through the following, ask yourself these questions and see what questions come to your mind, that you want to ask. Write them down using a yes/no format. You can also ask the example questions listed below regarding each of these laws or areas. Point to each main possibility with your index finger, while holding the pendulum with your other hand. Become a neutral witness, ask your question and record the response.

Example Questions:

- Is this law currently expressed in Elaine's life?
- Would Elaine benefit from paying more attention to this law?

1. ***Diet,*** sustains health and well-being in sixty percent of cultures. It has to do with the quality of mind, the beliefs and the attitudes (negative versus positive). Attitudes and thoughts track around health and positive beliefs ***Focus on what DID work!***

a. ***Diet of Mind:*** Are your memories and thoughts predominately positive? Do you focus on what has worked well for you, producing happiness during the day. Do you look at what did not work for you only briefly?

b. ***Emotional Diet:*** What ways do you support your emotional health? Do you pursue activities that totally nurture you that you can do for yourself? Do you experience self- respect? Do have experience self- love? Do you know what has heart and meaning for you personally? What do you imagine as your highest future emotional nature?

c. ***Spiritual Diet:*** What is your spiritual reality? Do you talk to God or Spirit in prayer? Do you meditate and listen to spiritual guidance? Do you allow sacred time to find a deeper sense of who you are? Are you happy with what your spiritual biography looks like? Do you know what food for the soul, means to you? Do you know what is sacred to you?

d. ***Physical Diet:*** Is your relationship to foods of different kinds healthy? Often the foods we were raised with are healing or comfort foods. Aromas with childhood memories can be healing. Every culture has its own healing soup.

2. Do you exercise to sustain your health? Do you do inner exercises which have meaning for you? Have you ever participated in rites of passage? Consider the following:

a. ***Birth:*** relates to what is new right now, an announcement of something being born, new people or friends, how do you experience it? Fear? Curiosity? Consider having 12 birthdays a year on your birth date. Do something new that you have never done before on that date.

b. ***Entry:*** relates to how you make contact with others, including greeting rituals such as hugs, handshakes, eye contact or bowing. All cultures make masks of changing identities. Keys, masks, doors and windows are symbols for making contact.

c. ***Initiation:*** relates to your willingness to learn something new and to demonstrate that you have learned it. Initiation reflects where you are currently being tested and challenged. Look at who or what is your current teacher, (positive or negative)? Initiation dreams include going to school, books, garments and processes of exposure.

d. ***Marriage or Merging:*** relates to the outer party. What does it mean to you internally? What about merging, polarizing, synergy, synthesis, conflict resolution and negotiation. Our culture seldom takes time out for merging. Changes take a full year or two for adjustment to these experiences. Do you take time to integrate and process? Do you possess the needed commitment for marriage?

e. ***Demonstration:*** indicates the way shower, the healer, the teacher who shares with others, the important stranger. Look at who the facilitators are in your life. Do you effectively demonstrate what you know and feel?

f. ***Attainment:*** relates to no longer needing to learn something or demonstrate it. You model it just by being. You no longer need to study it or teach it. You no longer need to defend your position, it's a place beyond ego, with nothing to prove. It's a state of contentment. Dreams of contentment often include light or rose colored windows, gems, gifts or relaxation in nature.

g. ***Death:*** relates to the process of letting go and releasing, ending and completing. Long extended good-byes are often symbolic of this rite of passage. When you look at death, you realize it indicates that whatever you complete will create space for something new to happen. The Universe cannot stand in a void. The only thing consistent with life is change. Completion is a means to a beginning. All cultures ritualize death. We can also ritualize what we have outgrown. Trees are symbols of death and rebirth. Fall represents completion and letting go. Winter is incubation or assimilation. Spring is birth and new beginnings, and Summer is fruition and abundance.

3. ***Humor:*** all cultures realize humor can help to sustain health. Laughter acts as a healing medicine in the body. How much laughter and humor is there in your life? What is the quality of humor and play in your life?

4. ***Music:*** this universal language has healing power. All cultures have songs of healing power. What kinds of music are the most healing for you? Do you take time to do nothing else but attune to the healing music of your choice?

5. ***Important people:*** relates to your support systems. Who are your support systems? With whom do you share mutual positive regard? Who would you like to have at your death bed? Who nurtures, loves and supports you? What non-nurturing systems do not support your health and well-being? Family? Government agencies? Legal systems? Is there an equal balance between your nurturing and being nurtured? Love is both receiving and extending. Do you block on receiving? With whom? When ill, you must receive. Is it easy for you to ask for help? Do you believe that love is the willingness to support the deep spiritual growth of another human being? Do you understand that touching is a basic human need, both internally and externally?

6. ***Environment:*** nature and the outdoors assists in sustaining your health. Can you stay depressed outdoors? Do you spend at least one hour outdoors each day? How healing is your home environment? Which room contains the most healing energy? What colors do you find the most healing? Color and beauty are healing. How healthy is your internal environment? Do you have self-love, respect and trust? Why or why not? Do you realize that getting into the opposites of these qualities makes you ill? Do you see that your self trust is in proportion to how much you trust others? Are you your greatest critic? Do you inflate yourself? Do you put yourself down? Do you recognize confidence in yourself as the ability to confide in yourself? Are you self- honest?

7. ***Meaningful service:*** Do you feel that you make a difference? Do you have positive on-going interests? Do you take time to contemplate and pursue your interests, hobbies and creativity? How do you lose or waste time? Do you create timeless moments that really count? Look at what you did alone between the ages of four and twelve to get an idea of what you can do as an adult for the childlike feeling of timelessness.

8. ***Transpersonal:*** Do you accept or contemplate the mysteries of life? Do you have specific ways that you relate to that which is sacred? Do you accept life as it is? Can you forgive the past and move on? Do you experience the power of acceptance and being accepted?

What questions are you inspired to ask? List additional ones in a yes/no answer format and use your pendulum to observe what your unconscious believes is true!

Obsessive-Compulsive Disorders

Obsessions are persistent, distressing, unwanted thoughts or impulses that are senseless and irresistible. Compulsions are acts resulting from obsessions. Obsessive-compulsive disorder is a chronic or recurring illness, dominated by obsessions and compulsions. This condition is far less common than panic disorder. Both sexes are affected equally. Point to each possibility with your index finger, while holding the pendulum with your other hand. Become a neutral witness, ask your question and record the response.

Example Questions:

- Is this obsession currently a problem for Jerry?
- Has this obsession been a problem for Jerry in the past?
- Does Jerry have an inherent tendency towards this fear?
- Is Jerry's current obsession related to his church?
- Is Jerry making progress to move beyond this obsession ?
- Did Jerry's current obsession begin between 1967-1987?
- Is Jerry's current obsession past life related?

Write your questions, using the name of the person in question.

Obsessive-Compulsive Disorders

Panic disorder

Obsessional ideas

Obsessional images

Obsessional convictions

Obsessional ruminations (prolonged, inclusive thinking about a subject to the exclusion of other interests.)

Obsessional impulses

Obsessional fears

Obsessional rituals

Prescription Drug Dangers

Pendulum divination can be a vital tool for reducing or eliminating the dangers of using or mixing prescription drugs. Consider the following from Thomas J. Moore, George Washington University, one of the leading experts on prescription drug dangers:

- "An estimated 100,000 people die each year from prescription drug causes: adverse reactions, side effects, allergic reactions, drug interactions, physician prescription errors or patient mistakes.
- Prescription drugs kill more people each year than automobile and airplane accidents combined.
- One million people annually-one in four over a lifetime- will be hospitalized due to adverse effects of a prescription drug. A Food and Drug Administration survey of consumers shows 70% of physicians don't tell patients about the adverse side effects of drugs they prescribe.
- Taking prescription drugs must be considered serious business. You must realize that each drug has its risks and benefits. You must learn about these risks and benefits so you can use drugs wisely and protect yourself from unnecessary adverse effects.
- Make yourself an active partner in your medical care. Take questions and issues of concern to your doctor-and insist on answers. Also take advantage of the enormous knowledge pharmacists have about adverse effects of drugs.
- Keep a medical register, including the brand and chemical names of the drugs you're taking...why you're taking them...the doses and times you're taking them...and any questions you have about possible adverse effects or combinations. Review your medical register with your physician and pharmacist often."

You may choose to get a second opinion with pendulum divination. You can ask questions about adverse side effects or about combining any drugs or alcohol to insure your safety.
Point to each question with your index finger, while holding the pendulum in your other hand. Become a neutral witness, ask your question and record your response.

Example Questions: (You may touch the bottle or the drug name.)

- Is it currently in Edith's best interest to take this medication along with these sleeping pills?
- Is it currently in Edith's best interest to take this medication along with one half of this sleeping pill?
- Would Edith's liver or heart be at risk by taking these medications together?
- Is this drug causing Edith's skin to itch?
- Has taking this drug with alcohol caused an adverse reaction for this person?

Sexually Transmittable Diseases

We live in a world of AIDS and HIV which kill and cause untold suffering. For your health and saftey, consider the questions below before sexual involvement. Remember, that it is best to use your own name when asking about yourself. Point to each possibility with your index finger, while holding the pendulum with your other hand. Become a neutral witness, ask your question and record the response.

Herpes Progenitalis
Hepatitis
Syphilis
Gonorrhea
Chancroid
Molluscum contagiosum
Donovanosis
Tricomoniasis
Lymphogranuloma venereum
Monilial vagenitas
Pediculosis pubis (crabs)
Condyloma acuminata (genital warts)
AIDS

Example Questions:

- Is it in C.J.'s best interest to insist that Phil gets a blood test?
- Does C.J. currently have this problem? (Your mind already knows you are asking about the specific disease as you point to it, even if you add one, say a communicable disease, like strep)
- Has this disease been a problem for C.J. in the past?

Write your questions in a yes/no format, using your name and the name of the other person in question.

Uncovering Medical Challenges with Body Scanning

You can use your pendulum and ask specific questions regarding any part of any person's body, including your own. You can do this in two ways:

1. You can touch the body in question with one hand and work the pendulum with your other hand.
2. You can use a map or picture of the body part. A copy of ***any*** medical books with good illustrations can be used. I suggest, Price's Textbook of the Practice of Medicine (Oxford Univ. Press), as a professional medical text covering the description, diagnosis, and treatment of virtually every known disease or illness.

Pendulum divination will work even if:

1. the person you are working with is unconscious
2. you do not know the names of the body parts you are asking about
3. you are working with children who can't talk
4. you are working with people who speak a different language
5. the sample you are using is old, such as dried blood

Using illustrations is especially important if:

1. the desired information is related to a person who is not present
2. you need to communicate the problem to health care providers
3. the problem is internal

Because our minds and souls are connected to everything and everyone and we know what we are asking about, our divination will be accurate even if we don't know how to spell the name of the body part or don't know what it is called! Merely pointing to an illustration, body part or sample works! Diagnosing in this non-invasive and totally humane way also works with pets and animals of every sort using the same procedures. (see page 54)

Dowsing Process for Medical Questioning

1. Look at the sample questions and prepare one that fits the current situation
2. Be sure to use the person's name that you are asking about
3. When asking about yourself, use your name, rather than my
4. Touch the actual body part, picture of it or sample, with one hand
5. Hold the pendulum with your other hand
6. Become a neutral witness and receive the neutral/vertical movement
7. Ask your questions, one at a time
8. Record each answer

Asking questions such as,

•Is this the part of <u>Heather's</u> body which is causing her pain?

Fine-tune your questioning by using a list of possible conditions.

Example Questions:

•Are <u>Heather's</u> kidneys infected?

•Are <u>Heather's</u> kidneys swollen?

•Are <u>Heather's</u> kidneys toxic?

•Is <u>Heather's</u> left kidney punctured?

Use the same technique to check the individual systems of the body. Insert the <u>proper name</u> and use the list below.

Example Questions:

- Is____________ skeletal system in good health?
- Is____________ muscular system in good health?
- Is____________ nervous system in good health?
- Is____________ digestive system in good health?
- Is____________ cardio-vascular system in good health?
- Is____________ endocrine system in good health?
- Is____________ immune system in good health?
- Is____________ lymphatic system in good health?
- Is____________ excretory system in good health?
- Is____________ reproductive system in good health?

If you receive a negative response, you can fine-tune by asking more questions about specific body parts, such as the spine or right knee.

Your responses can provide a valuable second opinion and point medical professionals in the right direction if needed. You can use the following lists and generate meaningful questions of your own. You can easily locate illustrations or lists for any medical condition not included here! You can then use lists of possible treatments or medications to discern the most favorable course of action or treatment. (see page 67)

Investigative Techniques

"www.arttoday.com"

Longitude and Latitude Alignments

Divination with maps is an effective method for locating missing persons, aircraft, fires or other points of interest. It has been reported that military superpowers have used divination with maps for locating submarines and various other military applications.

The intriguing thing about the mind is, it doesn't matter if you can spell the location or the person's name! If you are clear about what you want to know, or who you want to know about, you will still be accurate! This has been incredibly valuable in my investigative location work, when phone callers don't always have accurate details, such as, spelling of locations or age of lost persons. You can use the following investigative process to locate anyone or anything, such as stolen property.

1. Locate the appropriate map.
2. To locate the latitude (the angular distance North and South, the width-wise or horizontal dimension), begin moving your pendulum from the right top corner, moving downward in small segments, while asking a question regarding longitude location.

Example Question: Is this the latitude where Tyrel's plane is located?

3. Mark the map when you get a positive response.
4. Locate the longitude (the angular distance East and West, the lengthwise or vertical dimension), begin by moving your pendulum from the right bottom corner, moving left in small segments, while asking a question regarding latitude location.

Example Question: Is this the longitude where Tyrel's plane is located?

5. Mark the map when you get a yes response.
6. Locate the intersecting cross points or precise location.
7. You may then wish to use larger scale maps to fine-tune for location. State, county, city, or street maps may be appropriate.

Specific Questions for Fine-tuning

I have used the pendulum to locate people in adverse weather conditions. I have also frequently used it to locate missing teenagers!

Example Questions:

- Is Tyrel's plane covered in snow?
- Is Tyrel's plane under the water in the South Pacific?
- Is Rick staying at Aaron's house?
- Is Rick camping near McCall?
- Has Tonya been kidnapped?
- Is Tonya currently in a safe place?
- Is Tonya's intention to come home?
- Is Tonya being held against her will?

Locating Missing Funds Within a Company

Pendulum divination has been used to point company executives to the right department or person in my investigative work. You can ask about each company location, department or person. With practice you could become an excellent investigator. Use lists or maps to ask your specific questions.

Example Questions:

- Is this person currently stealing funds from ABC Company?
- Is this person currently using ABC Company funds with integrity?
- Is our L.A. location currently misusing funds from ABC Company?

There are many other security issues which are also very important. Can you think of others which are applicable to your business situation? (see Resources- pages 113-114)

Write your questions, using the name of the person, company and location in question.

Locating Missing or Hidden Objects and Persons

Next time you lose something important like your keys, contact lens, or child, use a pendulum to help you locate it! You can start by determining the direction. You can turn in a circle and ask if the object or person lies in this direction, continuing until the correct direction is found (see example, page 13). You can also ask specific questions which seem logical or use your intuition and format yes/no questions.

Example Questions:

- Is Matt's son out in this direction that I am facing?
- Are Matt's keys in the kitchen?
- Are Matt's keys in the bedroom?
- Is Matt's contact lens in a pocket of clothing?
- Are Matt's sunglasses in his briefcase?
- Was Matt's car borrowed by his brother?
- Will Matt's stolen property be returned?
- Will Matt's stolen property be returned by Monday?
- Is Matt's stolen car in New York City?

You can use maps to locate persons or objects in order to fine-tune the desired location within a specific state, city, street or building. Do your best to practice locating unimportant items first to hone your ability to remain neutral when you lose something of importance.

Write your own questions using a yes/no format, considering who, what, where and when.

Psychometry Exercise

Psychometry is the skill of picking up energies and vibrations from objects and getting intuitive feelings, sounds or mental pictures. This technique is often used when logical information is unavailable. Psychometry and telepathy are possible because of the oneness that exists at the subconscious and superconscious levels (soul levels).

Psychometry Exercise:

Breathe deeply and relax as you go into neutrality or trance. Pick up the object and feel it with both hands. Imagine becoming one with the object and notice your impressions. You can hold the object with one hand and use your pendulum with your other hand.

Swinging your pendulum neutrally, while holding your object, will assist you in concentrating and allowing the responses. You can ask questions and then later confirm the answers with your pendulum.

Telepathy Exercise:

1. Think of someone you wish to contact telepathically. This can work even if the person you wish to contact is no longer living. For confirmation, it is recommended that you choose someone whom you feel close to who is currently living and able to call you.
2. Create a clear connection by doing one or more of the following:
   - writing their name down
   - getting a picture of them
   - getting something that they hand wrote
   - getting something that belongs to them, preferably something that they have worn.
3. Breathe deeply and relax as you go into neutrality or trance, holding the name or object of this person.
4. Swing your pendulum over the article and say outloud,

Example Requests and Statements:
When receiving or giving for yourself use your name or I.

*(clockwise pendulum movement)
Elaine, please call Iris, Elaine, please call Iris now!
I, Iris, now choose to send forgiveness, understanding and love to Elaine.

*(counterclockwise pendulum movement)
I, Iris, now choose to receive a response from Elaine.
I, Iris, now ask to receive impressions from Elaine.
I, Iris, now ask to receive impressions from this object.

"Goodness, integrity and wisdom already exist within your spirit, but you must learn to access that consortium of wisdom."

Lynn V. Andrews, Love And Power

Personal Enrichment

Astrology, Planetary Insights

Astrology offers insights regarding the influences of the planets upon human affairs and events by correlating their positions and aspects to a person's precise time of birth. Using a pendulum, we can easily gain insights without referring to a completed astrological chart. Below is a list of planetary energies which can be used to discern if you are deficient or overwhelmed in any of these areas.

Example Questions:

- Is Jessica currently deficient in this influence?
- Is Jessica currently overwhelmed by this influence?

Sun	Principle of will, purpose, the urge to be
Moon	The subconscious mind, memory, the principles of formation of habits
Mercury	Logical thinking, the ability to communicate mentally
Venus	The principal of attraction, the urge to relate to others socially and through the affections.
Mars	Physical energy, courage, the urge to do on the physical level
Jupiter	The urge to expand on every level
Saturn	The principle of discipline, order, time measurement, efficiency and limits
Neptune	The urge to envision a more perfect state of affairs; spiritual ideals, impersonal love and devotion
Uranus	Originality, the urge to the new and modern; the need to break through old traditions and manifest one's uniqueness.
Pluto	The urge to eliminate and transform that which is harmful to the organism

Astrology, Rising Sign Insights

Rising signs must be calculated with the exact time of birth unless you use a pendulum. To understand the influence of a rising sign refer to any basic astrological text. Rising signs may be discerned with pendulum divination by inserting the correct name, pointing to each astrology sign and asking:

Example Questions:

- Is this Gary's rising sign?
- Will Mary's baby have this rising sign?

Aries	Libra
Taurus	Scorpio
Gemini	Sagittarius
Cancer	Capricorn
Leo	Aquarius
Virgo	Pisces

The houses in astrology embody certain qualities, lessons or opportunities. You may use your pendulum to obtain guidance regarding karmic strengths or fears within each house or segment.
If you discover an area of difficulty, you may wish to fine-tune, asking specific questions about each aspect of the house. A chart of the houses is on the following page.

Example Questions:

- Does Victoria currently have any strengths associated with this house?
- Does Victoria currently have any fears associated with this house?
- Fine-tuning for fears, example, 5th house:
- Does Victoria currently have any fears associated with creativity?
- Does Victoria currently have any fears associated with children?
- Does Victoria currently have any fears associated with speculation?
- Does Victoria currently have any fears associated with love affairs?
- Are Victoria's fear about love affairs past life related?
- Are Victoria's fear about love affairs related to her parents?
- Is it currently beneficial for Victoria to ask questions regarding medical astrology?

Astrology, House Insights

Affirmation Example:

I have found it very important to focus on our challenges and get clear about what we want with affirmations. You may wish to write your own affirmations and imagine integrating them with the counterclockwise movement. The following is an example of affirmations for the 5th house.

- I, Victoria am naturally creative. My creativity has endless avenues for positive expression.
- I, Victoria accept the responsibilities and joys of sharing with children.
- I, Victoria understand the value of studying, weighing, balancing and speculating. I trust my ability to integrate all reasoning and intuition properly, for the highest good of all concerned.
- I, Victoria now choose to accept healing and forgiveness for all hurts and fears associated with love affairs, and as a result, I trust that I am now able to love and accept love unconditionally.

Direct and Worthy Goals

Often my clients come to see me with very clear thoughts, actions, feelings and descriptions of what they don't want. Since like attracts like and energy follows thought, it's a challenge not to create more of the same unwanted dramas. Therefore, I guide them to **become clear about what they do want.**

I also assist them in becoming sure that their goals are worthy of achievement. Often we think that things such as a new job, car, house or relationship will be what we want and need. However, we must ask ourselves, **"what will having this give me that is positive and how will I feel when I have achieved this goal?"** Asking this question helps us acknowledge if the goals we seek are worthy of attainment and may give us ideas about how to get our needs met more directly and easily.

Some of our goals are unrealistic, like wanting everyone to be kind and grateful to us or not wanting to make any mistakes in life. Our goals may be the reflection of an unwanted attitude or belief structure. Often, the sacrifices, efforts and risks required to achieve these unrealistic goals may make them not worthy of attaining. Many people still feel unsatisfied even when they obtain unrealistic goals! They discover that this goal is not what they really want after all. When people are driven to gain power, fame or great fortune it is usually because they believe it will make them feel secure, lovable, respected or satisfy some other very basic need. We will explore some important questions that can lead you to discover more satisfying and worthwhile goals.

1. Consider these areas listed below and write down some of your goals in a positive format.

personal	business	relationship
physical	educational	spiritual

Positive goals that I want are:

2. What will having *this goal* do or get for me that's positive?

If I had *this goal*, I would feel more______________________________

loved safe creative

If I had *this goal*, I would have more______________________________

security, self-awareness, self-respect, personal time

If I had *this goal*, I would experience______________________________

new relationships, new environments, more fun at work

Is there an easier or more direct way to get this need or goal met?

You can use your pendulum to ask if each of these statements is true for you and fine-tune your own questions for more accuracy.

Secondary Gain

Secondary gain is a term used by therapists to indicate the hidden pay offs and agendas which lurk behind unwanted behaviors. As a hypnotherapist, I want to present an exercise for secondary gain, because I believe that **all of our needs are positive. When we discover the need behind the behavior and treat it as positive, we can more efficiently find other ways to get our needs met.**

Replacing a negative habit (thought, action or feeling) with something positive always reinforces easy, positive change. Not only does it assist filling the void, it adds new, positive elements. Gaining clarity about our payoffs for unwanted behaviors is very important. Knowing what we do want to create is also vital to the healing process.

Complete the following sentences, using the words below and adding your own to these lists.

1. **I have nothing to gain,** by being <u>(negative thought, action or feeling.)</u>

deprived	betrayed	depressed	self-destructive
lonely	overly critical	denied	sick
rejected	victimized	seperate	lazy

2. The positive need I have when I (<u>think critical thoughts or smoke intensely, or I feel lonely and rejected,</u>) is to feel (<u>confident, or to relax and let go, or to feel safe and accepted</u>.)

3. **I have nothing to lose,** by ______________________________

getting my needs met	being kind	being grateful	being honest
being self-compassionate	passionate	speaking my truth	being creative
doing my best	following my joy		
being motivated & confident	feeling safe and accepted		
trusting in myself	imagining the best		
praying for world peace	trusting in what I am good at		
feeling confident	relaxing and letting go......		

4. I have everything to gain by <u>(getting my needs met.)</u>

Example: I have nothing to gain by being, <u>destructive with my smoking habits.</u> The positive need I have when I smoke might be, <u>to feel the comfort of a friend, or to be alone, or to relax and let go.</u> I have nothing to lose by <u>gaining the comfort of friends, enjoying time alone, relaxing and letting go while I rest.</u>

Now use your pendulum to ask if each statement is true!

Example Question:

- Is this statement true for <u>Kate</u>?

Palmistry

As a professional palmist with twenty years of experience, I have encountered many awesome stories and confirmations about the accuracy of my consultations. Yes, your destiny and personality is written in your hands! Many medical aspects of palmistry have also been well documented. It is my experience that accuracy happens when both logic and intuition are responsibly blended with humility and compassion.

Our hands are truly the servants of our brain. The dexterity that allows us to perform even the simplest tasks without conscious thought is truly amazing. Our hands can tell a hundred interesting stories. The hands reflect the person and the palmist reflects the hands. Palmistry is both a science and an intuitive art form, culminating in the art of interpretation. Many great books are now available for the serious student (see resources, page 113). Although it may take one many years to gain proficiency in palmistry, I have included some basic divination exercises which enhance the giving and receiving capabilities of your glorious hands!

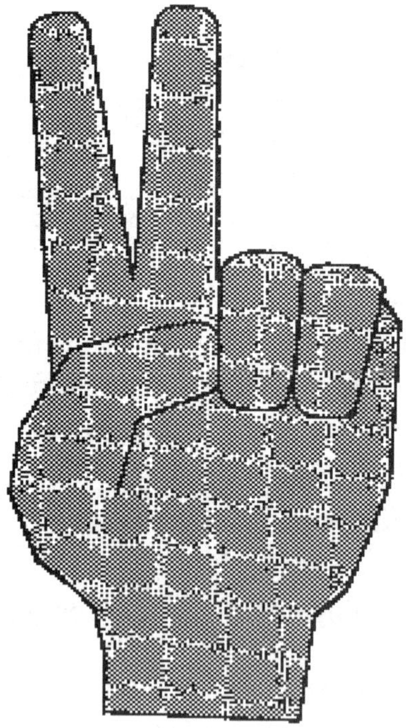

PEACE
According to palmistry,
a natural space between these two fingers indicates independence of thought, the ability to envision a future unlike the past. One NOT bound by traditions, creeds or dogmas.

Palmistry, Enhancing Your Lines and Seven Sacred Archetypes.

The lines on your hands are manifestations of energy, formed by the brain and through the nervous system. They are in a constant state of change. With pendulum divination techniques, you can choose to enhance these energies in each of your major lines and seven archetypes.

Major Lines

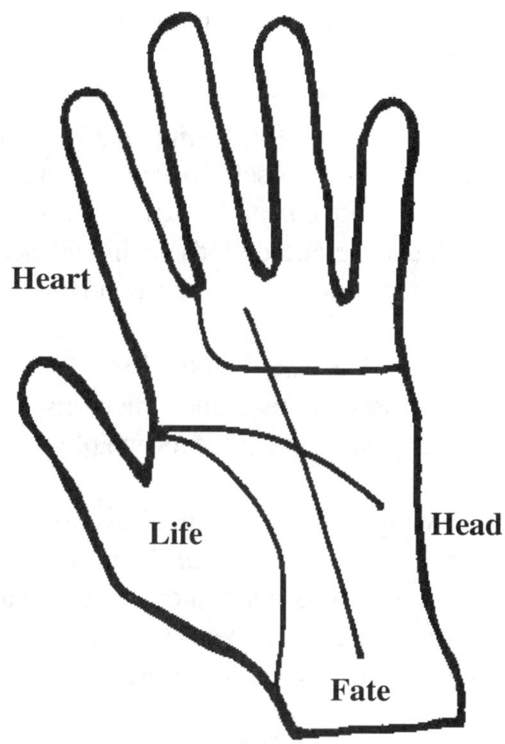

Seven Archetypes

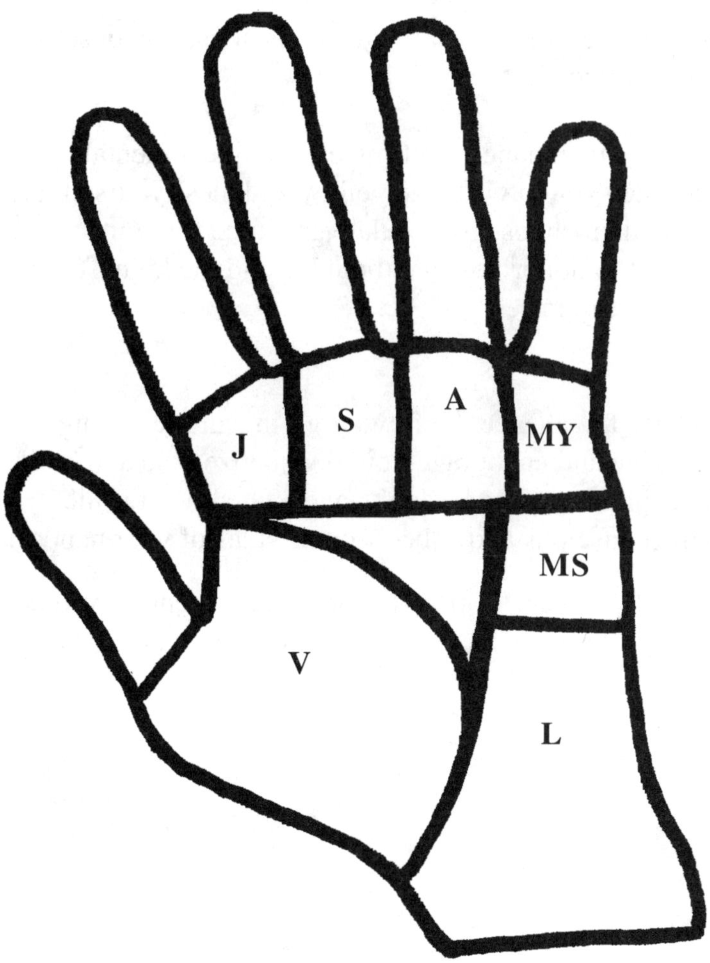

J- Jupiter **S- Saturn**
MS- Mars **L- Luna**

A- Apollo **MY- Mercury**
V- Venus

You can swing your pendulum above each line and ask a question or make an affirmative statement. What do you want to ask, give or receive? What do you want to attune to? What do you choose?

Possible Exercise- Heart Line

Locate your heart line which represents your emotional expression or repression. Your heart line represents the conscious, subconscious and superconscious aspects of your emotions and your physical heart's health indications.

Swing your pendulum above the line and ask to enhance the flow of loving energy. Ask to give and receive grateful, loving energy. I enjoy pink for the heart line and encourage you to visualize pink and bless yourself. You may then choose to receive and circulate the gratitude and love in a counter clockwise movement, and to honor love and the highest good for all concerned. You may then choose to circulate the gratitude and love in a clockwise movement. Sending it out to honor love and the highest good for all concerned which is wise and fun because it can create miracles!

Possible Exercise- Head Line

Locate your head line which represents your mental expression and will, conscious, subconscious and superconscious aspects and physical brain health indications.

Swing your pendulum above the head line and ask to enhance the flow of intelligent mental energy. I enjoy yellow for the head line, and encourage you to visualize yellow and bless yourself and others and all forms of mental expression. You may then choose to circulate gratitude for your intelligence in a clockwise movement and send it out to honor positive thoughts and the highest good for all concerned. Circulate gratitude because it can create miracles!

Possible Exercise- Fate Line

Swing your pendulum above the fate line and ask to enhance the flow of giving and receiving energy, the gift of destiny. I enjoy blue for the fate line and encourage you to visualize blue and bless yourself and others and all forms of ones destiny expression. If you don't have a fate line, it is the neutral or middle way that blends and balances the conscious and subconscious sides of your hands.

Swing your pendulum above the middle of the hand, palm up, from top to bottom in the neutral, vertical movement. Circulate gratitude for giving and receiving, because it creates miracles! What if creating miracles could be that simple?

Possible Exercise- Life Line

Locate your life line which represents your physical expression, health and timing, conscious, subconscious and superconscious aspects of timing and physical health indications.
Swing your pendulum above the life line and ask to enhance the flow of life and physical energy.
I enjoy green for the life line and encourage you to visualize the most beautiful green, or whatever color you prefer, and bless yourself and others and all forms of life's physical expression.

What if the truth is that we are all doing our best to pull it together to create harmony, and it takes just enough of us to create with just a little bit more awareness to assist us all in soul healing and manifesting the superconscious aspects of Spirit, Mind and Heart? What if your positive preferences demonstrate your self-love and enhance your spiritual guidance when you work or play with them?

What if. . .?

Seven Archetypes

You can choose to move your archetypal energy and enhance it through your mounts.
The mounts, which reflect the seven primary planetary archetypes on your hands, are manifestations of energy, formed in certain locations, (see chart page 93).

Possible Exercise- for Mounts (Jupiter, Saturn, Apollo, Mercury, Venus, Luna, or Mars)

Swing your pendulum above each mount and ask to enhance the flow of energy. You may pick qualities from the mounts listed on the next page and ask to gratefully give and receive honesty or any quality you choose. You may choose to imagine a favorite color, breathing deeply to enjoy a restful and grateful trance.
I encourage you to experience blessing yourself with your gratitude and love.
You can use the negative swing to release any possible negative influence and the positive swing to light up the void and enhance forward movement. You may choose to point to each quality and ask:

Example Questions:

- Is Kathleen currently deficient in this quality?
- Is Kathleen currently expressing this quality in a balanced way?
- Is Kathleen currently expressing to much of this quality?

Statements and Affirmation:

- I choose to honor and celebrate honesty (quality).
- I ask to attune to and receive my highest vibration of the Jupiter energy (see qualities listed below) for the highest possible good. (Pointing to Jupiter or focusing on your hands.)
- I ask to attune to and give my highest vibration of the Jupiter energy for the highest possible good.

Write your questions or statements, using your name in each question.

Jupiter

Positive qualities: warm, optimistic, honest, expansiveness, spirituality or religion, teaching, humanitarian endeavors, a sense of higher purpose and leadership qualities, lucky, sacred space and place, catalyst, teacher, politician or minister.

Possible negatives to eliminate or release:
misdirected power, dominance, negative use of positions of power, tyranny.
(the pointer finger of authority that clearly points out one's will!)

Saturn

Positive qualities: self control, caution, wisdom, mental, math, medicine, history, serious, introspective, studious, reclusive, cold, sciences, natural scenery and earth tones. Researchers, teachers, historians.

Possible negatives to eliminate or release: dislikes resistant, opinionated, suspicious, rebellious, morbid pessimist

Apollo

Positive qualities: warm, social, spontaneous, brilliant, dramatic, limelight, artistic, versatile, adaptable, sense of humor, resourceful, successful, arts, photography, flowers, beauty, design and creative harmony.

Possible negatives to eliminate or release: excessive need for recognition, arrogance, show off, prideful, boastful, need for loved ones to shine

Mercury

Positive qualities: physical and mental agility, warm, quick and skillful, dexterity, shrewd, communication skills, math, sciences, sports and games.

Possible negatives to eliminate or release: misuse of communication, schemer, manipulative, dishonest, negative game player

Venus

Positive qualities: warmth, compassion, family life, fellowship and connection, affectionate, generous, demonstrative, heart centered friend, animal and music lover, nurturer, forgiving and loyal companion, passionate

Possible negatives to eliminate or release: blinded by excessive emotional wanting, misguided desire or generosity, misguided passion, unrealistic emotional expectations

Luna

Positive qualities: imagination, evolved vocabulary and visualization skills, writing skills, cold, poetry, refined tastes, change, travel, water, intense, elusive, highly creative.

Possible negatives to eliminate or release: imaginary illness, hypercritical, selfish, restless, nervous, cold

Mars

Positive qualities: abundant health and strength, energetic, hot, ardent and determined, courageous, warrior, resistance to opposition and opinions of others, builder, sports, nature and hiking or trekking.

Possible negatives to eliminate or release: unconcerned, quarrelsome, bully, intense temper, violent, misdirected sexual passions, lascivious.

Power Places and Sacred Spaces

People all over the world go to special locations where they feel a strong personal connection with the power of nature. Some are drawn to the sea, some to the mountains and others to the desert.

Many people feel that nature's power places are sacred and can revitalize them on many levels. Sacred spaces and prayer can change your life by assisting in your attunement to your eternal soul. The shaman may create an altar, garden or circle of stones to symbolize and step into sacred space. Many wise teachers have encouraged us to seek those places that we resonate with and wish to bless and make them sacred places of power by praying or performing some kind of ritual. You, and every life form are connected to the sacred, eternal web of life!

What if your life can be a blessing, honoring blessings and blessing everything!
Can mental, emotional and spiritual evolution be that simple?
Can you be that simple?

Example Exercises:
When attuning, giving or receiving for yourself you can use your name or I.

* You may wish to use your pendulum to center yourself with the neutral vibration and become a silent witness while sitting on a rock or under a tree. Become a silent, neutral peace witness as you say <u>peace</u> and attune to this gift or essence.(neutral pendulum movement)
* You can use your pendulum to ask questions regarding the most beneficial places for meditation or contemplation.
* You can use your pendulum to send healing intentions (clockwise pendulum movement), to anywhere you are or can imagine yourself to be.
* Take your list of Spiritual Essences (page102) and your pendulum to a peaceful place in nature. Find yourself in a comfortable position and breathe fully and deeply as you ask to attune to, receive or give each essence.

Example Statements and Affirmations:

- I choose to *attune* to the essence of <u>Trust.</u>
  (neutral, vertical pendulum movement)
- <u>I, Iris,</u> now choose to lovingly and gratefully assist my soul healing, and the highest good of all by *attuning* to <u>Peace.</u> (neutral, vertical movement)

- I, Iris, allow the neutral movement and attune to Peace for the highest good of all concerned.
- I, Iris choose to ***receive*** and resonate with Balance. (counterclockwise pendulum movement)
- I, Iris gratefully ***give*** and resonate with Balance. (clockwise pendulum movement)
- I, Iris choose to enhance and ***give*** Freedom to all aspects of life. (clockwise pendulum movement)
- I, Iris, choose to ***give*** Peace for the highest good of all concerned. (clockwise pendulum movement)

Write your own questions and create your own prayers or rituals. Common rituals include dancing, singing and meditation.

How will you choose to participate in loving and intelligent co-creation and peacemaking?

Spiritual Laws

You can apply the skills of pendulum divination to the following spiritual principles adapted from the book, *"The Laws of Spirit"* by Dan Millman.

Point to each possibility with your index finger, while holding the pendulum with your other hand. Become a neutral witness, ask your question and record the response. Your answers will be anywhere from 1 to 10 positive or 1 to 10 negative. When receiving for yourself you can use your name or I. When giving of yourself, you can use your name or I.

Example Questions:

- •Is Elaine's current experience of this law deficient?
- •Is this law currently expressed in Elaine's life?
- •Will Elaine benefit from expecting miracles?

Example Statements:

- •I, Elaine, choose to receive and integrate the spiritual law of Balance.
- •I, Elaine, choose to receive and embody the quality of Balance.

THE LAW OF BALANCE
Finding the middle way, neutrality, centered, witnessing, allowing

THE LAW OF CHOICE
Free will, clear intentions, reclaiming your power, responses

THE LAW OF PROCESS
Taking life step by step, preparations, foundations, manifesting

THE LAW OF PRESENCE
Embracing the present moment, only now is real, inner peace, Divine timing

THE LAW OF COMPASSION
Awakening your humanity, Unconditional love, forgiveness, extending self- love.

THE LAW OF FAITH
Self love, trusting in spirit, inner knowing, creating with spirit (co-creation)

THE LAW OF EXPECTATION
Disciplined imagination, expecting miracles, prayer and contemplation, expanding your reality, Divine imagination

THE LAW OF INTEGRITY
Self monitoring, honoring your values, living your truth, expression of your internal reality

THE LAW OF ACTION
Self responsibility, courage, moving into life, permission to act, initiative

THE LAW OF CYCLES
Dancing natures songs, perfection, transformation, Divine right timing, cycling with the cosmic flow

THE LAW OF SURRENDER
Embracing Divine higher will, honoring your feelings, neutrality, turning it over to Spirit, looking for an open door, asking what's next

THE LAW OF UNITY
Remembering our connectedness, Oneness consciousness, higher truth, I am you, God drinking God

THE LAW OF LOVE
Embracing gratitude and freedom, joy and universal ideals, inspiration and service

Spiritual Qualities, or Essences.

You can choose to effect harmonious changes by repeating these essences and attuning to the oversoul (spiritual essence or vital force in the universe in which all souls participate, which transcends individual consciousness.)

You can choose to bring in and receive each essence with a counterclockwise or no movement. You can send out and give each essence with a clockwise or yes movement.
Example statements have been provided to assist you.

Example Questions:

- Is Patrick's current experience of this spiritual essence deficient?
- Is this soul quality currently expressed in Patrick's life?

Example Statements: Receiving & Giving

- I choose to ***receive*** and resonate with Balance. (counterclockwise)
- I choose to ***give*** and resonate with Balance. (clockwise)
- For the highest good of all concerned, I ask to honor and receive this spiritual essence now, Balance.
- For the highest good of all concerned, I ask to honor and give the spiritual essence of, Balance, sending it to my friend Stacie.

Say the word out loud and imagine the feelings associated with in it the universe. Say the words out loud and imagine the feelings associated with Balance in the universe and your loved one. You may wish to point to your friends name or picture.

Balance	Healing	Expectancy	Nurturing
Transformation	Trust	Truth	Communication
Integrity	Humor	Love	Light
Delight	Purpose	Power	Gratitude
Enthusiasm	Excellence	Blessings	Courage
Efficiency	Forgiveness	Honesty	Synchronicity
Play	Adventure	Surrender	Education
Freedom	Peace	Creativity	Grace
Loyalty	Understanding	Release	Beauty
Willingness	Openness	Simplicity	Purification
Abundance	Inspiration	Compassion	Responsibility
Consistency	Flexibility	Harmony	Wishes
Tenderness	Strength	Perfection	Brother/Sisterhood
Birth	Obedience	Tolerance	Clarity
Patience	Guidance	Brilliance	Mastery
Acceptance	Kindness	Service	Companionship

Starting Good Rumors

Starting good rumors is a blast! I first heard about a couple of college students who decided to pick someone to start a good rumor about who was unpopular and fairly unattractive. They wanted to learn more about self esteem. They each picked Jane. They each picked something positive that they sincerely felt was true about her. They began sharing some good rumors about her. Making comments like, Jane wears really nicely coordinated colors and she looks soft, I like that. I notice that Jane is really good at chemistry, I wonder if she would ever consider tutoring me? I really appreciate how beautiful Jane's hair looks in the sun. They were amazed as changes began to occur. The object of their rumors became more confident, friendly and popular. Each of their lives were transformed as they continued to spread good rumors and write about their findings and the new abundant good feelings.

What do you base your emotional intelligence on? If you reap what you sow, consider good rumors as a contribution to good karma and heartfelt miracles for everyone! A wise one once said, "Be sure of what you ask for, you just might get it, and never underestimate the power of your spoken word, your willingness or your intentions."

You may wish to make a list of names, (perhaps your children), and select one to spread good rumors about.

Example Question:

- Would Sylvia benefit from good rumors about her piano skills?
- Does Janet have natural skill for health care?
- Would Alisa benefit from good rumors about her animal care?
- Is encouraging Haley's storytelling abilities in her best interest?

Twelve Cycles of Truth

The Iroquois Peace Confederacy Tradition has handed down these twelve cycles of truth in honor of their peacemaking traditions.

You can ask questions regarding each cycle. Point to each possibility with your index finger while holding the pendulum with your other hand, become a neutral witness, ask your question and record the response.

Example Questions:

- Is Becky currently expressing this cycle?
- Is Becky currently resonating with this cycle in a balanced way?
- Would Becky benefit from focusing on this cycle now?

The Twelve Cycles of Truth are:

Learning the truth

Honoring the truth

Accepting the truth

Observing the truth

Hearing the truth

Presenting the truth

Loving the truth

Serving the truth

Living the truth

Working the truth

Walking the truth

Being grateful for the truth

Timing and Synchronicity

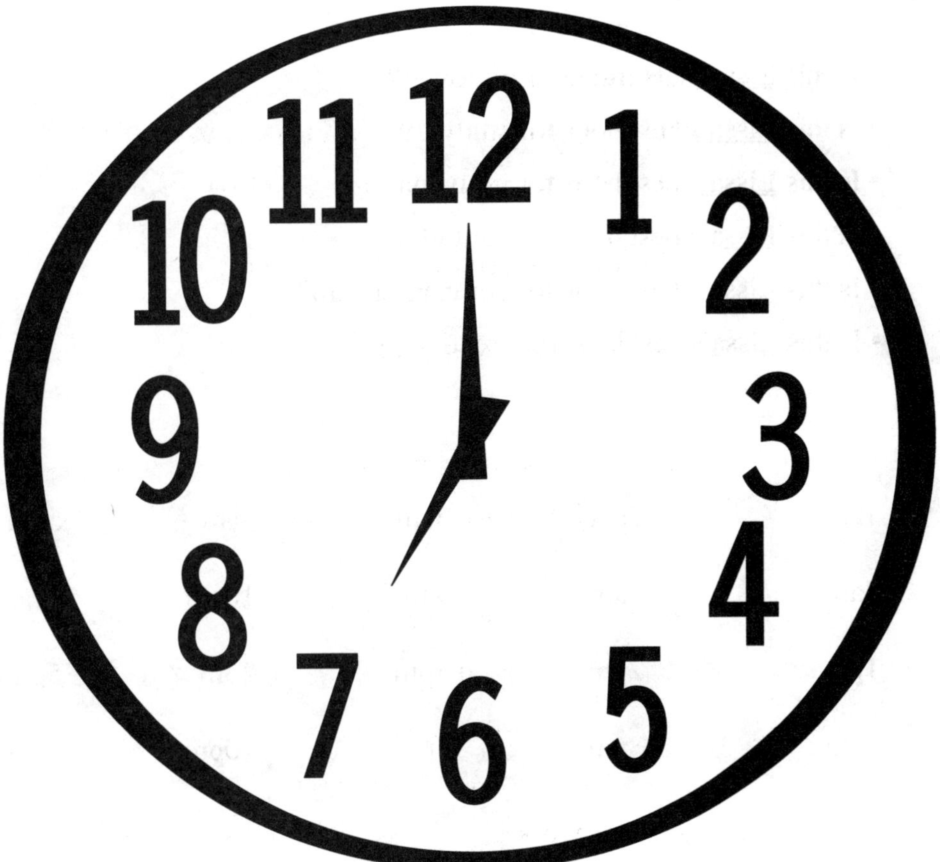

"www.arttoday.com"

Hour of Power

All human beings have their own internal timing and each person has an hour of power during a day's cycle. Each person feels more connection with a certain time of day. Your hour of power is your natural time of joy, education, rejuvenation or recreation. Some people feel a powerful connection to the hour they were born.

You may use your pendulum to discern your hour of power or someone else's. Ask your question while pointing to each hour.

Example Question:

- Is this Lissa's natural hour of power?
- Is this Lissa's best hour for study?
- Is this Lissa's best hour for rejuvenation?
- Is this Lissa's best hour for solitude?
- Is this Lissa's best hour for companionship?
- Is this Lissa's best hour for creative projects?

12am	1am	2am	3am	4am	5am
6am	7am	8am	9am	10am	11am
12pm	1pm	2pm	3pm	4pm	5pm
6pm	7pm	8pm	9pm	10pm	11pm

Timing and Synchronicity

Synchronicity is that amazing and miraculous timing of events that can leave us awestruck! Yes, timing is of the essence, and of vast importance in virtually every area of our lives. I once read that synchronicity was the oldest and most pervasive indication of spiritual guidance throughout history!

Remember that using timing words such as currently, now, in the past, in the near future, in the distant future, as well as asking about specific times and dates will assist your accuracy!

You can use your pendulum to discover the most beneficial or harmonious aspects of timing. You are encouraged to think about what aspects of timing are currently the most crucial in your life. The following example questions may serve as a catalyst to creating your own.

Example Questions:

- Will Patricia receive all of her back pay by next Friday?
- Will this check clear Patricia's bank by Friday?
- Is next week the most financially rewarding time to begin my advertising?
- Is it financially rewarding to begin my advertising after New Year's Day?
- Is it financially rewarding to stop my advertising until after New Year's Day?
- Is it in Suzanne's best interest to sign these documents today?
- Will Dina have her baby on the 8th?
- Will Dina's baby be born between 9am and 5pm?
- Will our dog have her puppies on Thursday before Dad gets home?

Months of the year

January	February	March	April
May	June	July	August
September	October	November	December

Days of the week

Monday	Tuesday	Wednesday	Thursday
Friday	Saturday	Sunday	

Hours of the day

12am	1am	2am	3am	4am	5am
6am	7am	8am	9am	10am	11am
12pm	1pm	2pm	3pm	4pm	5pm

My Favorite Synchronicity Story

I was in Park City, Utah in 1987 with my friend James, when he began complaining about his job and every aspect of it that he didn't like. I found myself preaching about the importance of focusing on the positive aspects of *what we do want to create, being optimistic and having a five year plan.* The next thing I said was, "I'll tell you where I'd like to be in five years. I'd like to have someone call me from a country that I've never worked in before and say that I was highly recommended, by someone from a different country and that they would like to send me money and questions in the mail to do some intuitive investigation work for them."

The next day, my phone rang while my friend James was there. It was a woman from a small town in France, saying that I was recommended by my client Leslie Williams, who was living in Brussels. She expressed interest in sending me some questions for investigation along with my fees! James just stared at me in shock! I said, "what did I say, five years, five days, or what?" We figured that it had been about twenty-five hours since I had stated this five year goal.

This experience reminded me of the importance of focusing on exactly what I do want, clearly and passionately asking for it and being gratefully aware of the synchronicity and timing as it unfolds!

I encourage you to think about how synchronicity manifests in your life!

Discover Your Skill and Accuracy

The following exercise is a fun opportunity to see how well you have grasped the basics of pendulum divination. You can check for accuracy on the following page. Below is a list of animals and some numbers indicating their gestation periods (how long it takes to grow them before they are born).

Point to each possibility (number of days) with your index finger, while holding the pendulum with the other hand. Become a neutral witness, ask your question and record the response.

Example Question:

Is this the correct gestation for <u>Bear</u>?

Bear
Dog
Camel
Cow
Cat
Deer
Elephant
Goat
Guinea Pig
Giraffe
Lion
Mare
Monkey
Opossum
Rabbit
Sheep
Sow
Squirrels
Fox

"www.arttoday.com"

"www.arttoday.com"

Length of Gestation for Animals:

21 days	26 days	28 days	30 days
62 days	108 days	112 days	8 weeks
9 weeks	5 months	6 months	7 months
8 months	9 months	11 months	11-12 months
14 months	21 months		

Check the answers on the next page for accuracy.

Answers: Gestation Time for Animals

Bear	6 months
Dog	9 weeks
Camel	11-12 months
Cow	9 months
Cat	8 weeks
Deer	8 months
Elephant	21 months
Goat	5 months
Guinea Pig	21 days
Giraffe	14 months
Lion	108 days
Mare	11 months
Monkey	7 months
Opossum	26 days
Rabbit	30 days
Sheep	5 months
Sow	112 days
Squirrels	28 days
Fox	62 days

"www.arttoday.com"

"www.arttoday.com"

CONCLUSION

The Future Is Yours

What does your future hold for you? No one can give you a complete answer to this question. Life presents too many variables and uncertainties. Even though you can not always predict the future, **you can** do certain things to insure its quality. You cannot control the future of the world, but **you can** control some of the events in your life and how you respond to them.

You can control your attitudes about the challenges you encounter and consciously participate in the directions of your faith and your soul's awakening and evolution. Remember, what you do today has a strong impact on what tomorrow holds for you.

Pendulum divination and exploration of alternative modes of consciousness will assist you in building a strong, positive, realistic path of action which will accompany you into the future. You are the one who will decide what gifts and blessings your divinity and divination hold for you.

The awakening to truth on the levels of divine knowing and communication technologies is a reality. I sense a great massive wake-up call soon, as high tech communication and consciousness combine to reveal Ultimate Truth. No more secrets, everyone can know the truth at all times. The positive use of shame (not living up to the standards of others), can lead us to new values and intentions that support ultimate wholeness.

Please continue to apply the teachings in this workbook to your own unique challenges and applications. Please continue to develop your self-trust, love and compassion as these qualities are truly the foundation of inner knowing. Believe in yourself, your soul and the sacred web of life which connects all sentient (alive, aware) souls of the great oneness. *Love, the dominating force of soul life, is in rapport with all souls and thus perpetuating the loving dance of life.* Imagine what our world could be like if we all decided to become the most loving, intelligent, creative, and aware beings that we can. Let your vision unfold; you are the visionary.

The future is yours.

Appendix

Bailey, Alice A. A Treatise on White Magic. Lucis Publishing Company.

Barratt, Iris K. Advanced Private Investigation Techniques. Awakening Visions Publishing, 1996.

Barratt, Iris K. Divination for Decision Makers. Awakening Visions Publishing, 1989.

Barratt, Iris K. Palmistry and Pendulum Divination Article. Awakening Visions Publishing, 1989.

Barratt, Iris K. Power of Forgiveness Cassette Tape. Awakening Visions Publishing, 1995.

Baylis, Janis, and Adrian Barthlow. Dowsing Dictionary. 1986.

Bird, Christopher. The Divining Hand. Schiffer Publishers Ltd.

Campbell, Linda. Multiple Intelligences Workshop. Simon and Schuster, 1993.

Jordan, Frank. Interview on Dowsing and Divination. 1998.

Meyer, Donna, and Deana. 30 Common Things Adults Say to Children Article, 1990.

Millman, Dan. The Laws of Spirit. HJ Kramer, 1995.

Moore, Thomas J. Prescription for Disaster. Simon and Schuster.

Nielsen, Greg. Pendulum Power. Destiny Books, 1987.

Tansley, David. Radionics, Science or Magic, A Holistic Paradigm of Radionic Theory and Practice. C.W. Daniel Publisher, 1982.

Woolf, Vernon V. PhD. Holodynamics. Harbinger House, 1990.

Resources

Graphics-
Art Today http:\\www.arttoday.com

The British Society of Dowsers
The Honorary Secetary
High Street Eydon Rugby
Warwickshire, England

The American Society of Dowersrs
PO Box 24
Danville, Vermont 05828

Resources

Canadian Society of Questers (Dowsing and Divination)
#22 2400 Oakdale Way
Kamloops, BC, V2B 6W7 Canada

Intuition Network, Institute of Noetic Sciences
475 Gate Five Road, Suite 300
Sausalito, CA 94965

Association for the Study of Dreams (ASD)
PO Box 1600
Vienna, VA 22183

A Conscious Person's Guide to Relationships, Ken Keys, Jr.
Living Love Publications

Addiction and Grace, by Gerald G May, Harper San Francisco

The Artist's Way: A Spiritual Path to Higher Creativity, Julia Cameron

Astrology for the Soul, by Jan Spiller, Bantam Books

Beyond Meditation: Real Healing, video instructional intensive
by Tom Pritscher, "Thou Art Inc" website, www.realhealing.com

Chakras: Energy Centers of Transformation, by Harish Johari

Clearing The Way To Higher Consciousness, by Frank Jordan (on chakras)
website, www.psi-tronics.com

The Complete Manual of Corporate and Industrial Security,
by Russell L Bintliff

Feel the Fear and Do it Anyway, by Susan Jeffers

Resources

From Acupressure to Zen: An Encyclopedia of Natural Therapies
by Barbara Nash

General Investigative Techniques, by Daniel Hughes

Heart of the Mind, by Connirae Andreas and Steve Andreas,
Real People Press

Intuition Workout, by Nancy Rosanoff, Boulder Creek, CA: Aslan

Medical Astrology, by Eileen Nauman, Blue Turtle Publishing

Natures 12 Magic Healers: The Amazing Benefits of Cell Salts,
by Lionel Rolfe and Nigey Lennon

The Oracle Within, by Dick Sutphen, Pocket Books

The Oracle Divining/Healing Kit and Pendulum Divining Kit
www.psi-tronics.com

Pathways to Peace: Forty Steps to a Less Violent America,
by Victor LaCerva, Heartsong Publications

Personhood: The Art of Being Fully Human, by Leo Buscaglia,
Fawcett Columbine

The Power of Affirmations, by Jerry Frankhauser, Coleman Graphics

Practicing the Presence: A Course in Meditation, by Tom Pritscher
"Thou Art Inc." website, www.realhealing.com

Psychic Criminology: An Operations Manual for Using Psychics in Criminal Investigations, by
Whitney S. Hubbard and Raymond W. Worring

Seeing Past the Edge, by David Yurth

Soul Moments: Marvelous Stories of Synchronicity, by Phil Cousineau

Index

U

V

W

Y

"Any sufficiently developed technology is indistinguishable from magic."

Arthur C. Clarke

In Addition to the Divination Workbook, IRIS K. BARRATT CHT,
also offers these professionally recorded Self-Hypnosis tapes and CD's.

ORDER FORM

Please send the following...

ITEM	HOW MANY	PRICE
The Divination Workbook- $24.95 ea.		
Self Hypnosis Cassette Tapes- $12.95 ea. **CD's - $15.95 ea.**		
Attracting Your Soul Mate (gender non-specific)		
Stop Smoking Forever		
Weight Loss and Exercise Motivation		
Discover Your Souls Purpose		
Creating Prosperity and Gratitude		
Discovering Your Guardian Angel		
Study Skills and Exam Success		
Pain Management		
Eliminate Insomnia		
Generating New Choices and Behaviors		
Forgiveness of Self and Others		
Personal and Planetary Peace		
Pre and Post Surgical Success		
Idaho residents please add 5% sales tax		
Please add $1.50 per tape and CD or $3.00 per book for shipping and handling.	Shipping and Handling	
	TOTAL	

Please ship to:
Name
Address
City, State, Zip
Telephone

Please mail orders to:
Awakening Visions, PO Box 80 Bellevue, ID 83313 USA
Website www.awakeningvisions.com
Fax (208) 788-8585

EMAIL<Ourgoddessiris@juno.com>

About the Author

Rev. Iris K. Betts-Barratt CHT, CMT, is a minister, certified clinical hypnotherapist, massage therapist, palmistry expert, and professional clairvoyant investigator with 20 years experience. She is also a highly respected peace activist and teacher of spiritual principles. Iris is a long time Idaho resident, living near Sun Valley. She is the author of Divination for Decision Makers, as well as many articles on divination, dowsing, investigation techniques, forgiveness, hypnotherapy, palmistry and peacemaking. Iris' unique talents and spiritual orientation have put her in demand internationally as a teacher, lecturer and private consultant. She has devoted over two decades to the study of divination, the workings of the soul and spiritual guidance. Her primary goals in life are to be a channel of blessings, a healing presence, and the most grateful person she knows. Her passion is enhancing educational and cultural diversity, as well as teaching investigative techniques around the world.

Iris is a trustee of Planet Peace, a non-profit organization, dedicated to the research and development of global healing. Reverend Barratt is also a volunteer board member for The Interfaith Peacemaking Resource Center of Utah.

Iris offers many workshops to provide personal and global empowerment. She is a highly respected therapist and visionary peacemaker who believes that when we practice forgiveness in any area of our lives, we move from divisiveness and war (with others and within ourselves) to reconciliation, resolution and peace.

Iris is a volunteer for Blaine Manor where she provides massage therapy for her local elders. She is a loving mother and involved member of her community. She is grateful to be of service locally and internationally.

Iris K Barratt would love to hear from you!

If this book or any other work of the author has made a difference in your life or if you have ideas you would like to contribute, please take a moment and let her know. Send all correspondence to the address below:

Rev. Iris K Barratt
PO Box 80
Bellevue, Idaho 83313 USA
Fax: +1 208 788-8585

EMAIL<Ourgoddessiris@juno.com>